The Judicious Professor

*A Learner-Centered
Philosophy
for Teaching
and Learning
in Higher Education*

*Paul Gathercoal
& Forrest Gathercoal*

Caddo Gap Press

i

The Judicious Professor
A Learner-Centered Philosophy
for Teaching and Learning in Highger Education

Paul Gathercoal and Forrest Gathercoal

Published by
   Caddo Gap Press
   3145 Geary Boulevard PMB 275
   San Francisco, California 94118 U.S.

Price $29.95 US

ISBN 1-880192-53-5

Library of Congress Cataloging-in-Publication Data

Gathercoal, Paul.
   The judicious professor : a learner-centered philosophy for teaching and learning in higher education / Paul Gathercoal & Forrest Gathercoal.
      p. cm.
   Includes bibliographical references.
   ISBN 1-880192-53-5 (alk. paper)
   1. College teaching. 2. Effective teaching. 3. Educational psychology. 4. Learning, Psychology of. I. Gathercoal, Forrest. II. Title.
   LB2331.G38 2007
   378.1'2—dc22
                              2006100681

Contents

Acknowledgments iii

Introduction 1

Chapter One
The Ethics of a Healthy Teaching
and Learning Relationship 7

Chapter Two
Learning, Motivation, and Goals 25

Chapter Three
A Constitutional Perspective 43

Chapter Four
Establishing Mutual Goals and Expectations 63

Chapter Five
Judicious Consequences—
A Professional Responsibility Model 79

Contents

Chapter Six
A Synthesis and Evaluation
of Legal, Ethical, and Educational Issues 105

Chapter Seven
Judicious Prudence: Ideology and Politics 159

Appendix I
The Brain and Cognition, Affect, and Behavior 166

Appendix II
Are You Perceived as a Judicious Professor? 209

References 221

About the Authors 225

Acknowledgments

For our parents,

Paul and Marion Gathercoal

We want to acknowledge and thank those who have been influential in helping us write and develop the philosophy and complementary dialogic approaches to teaching and learning in higher education that epitomize *The Judicious Professor*.

We owe a great debt of thanks and gratitude to our wives, Gwen and Joan, and our children, Bob, Erin, Justin, and Susie, for their love and support during our continuous process of becoming and developing *The Judicious Professor*. We also want to thank our extended family and in particular our sister, Peggy Poling, Ed.D., who provided us with precious feedback on our writing and organization of the book.

Thank you, Alan H. Jones, Ph.D. You have been steadfast in your support for this philosophy at all levels of education and we are grateful to Caddo Gap Press for publishing and disseminating the book and enhancing the look and feel these ideas bring to the literature.

Grateful thanks are due to those who took the time to read and comment on the language, structure, and organization of *The Judicious Professor*. Thank you:

Luanne Stevenson Crockett, M.S. in Chemistry,
James Hand, M.S.,
Richard Jensen, Ed.D.,
Vern Jones, Ph.D.,
Douglas O. Love, Ph.D.,
Nancy Myers, M.A.,
Frank Nausin, M.Div.,

for your written feedback, critical eye, and judicious comments on our work. Without this feedback we work blind. You keep our senses genteel and our language fresh.

Finally, we thank our teachers, our students, and our colleagues who have worked with us through the years and who have given innocently of themselves and their ideas. Tacitly or deliberately these "colleagues in teaching and learning" have helped us to be what we are today. We owe our teachers and professors, our colleagues, and our students a great debt of thanks. It is a fun ride, thank you all.

Introduction

A common debate among educators is the age-old question as to whether teaching and learning is an "art" or a "science." Most textbooks addressing educational psychology begin with a discussion of these two approaches, arguing the merits of each and which one is more valuable to the teaching and learning process. The conclusion reached by most is that teaching and learning has both "artistic" and "scientific" aspects; because the "art" emphasizes personal qualities like inspiration, intuition, talent, and creativity and the "science" emphasizes a repertoire of techniques, procedures, and skills needed to convey the curriculum in a systematic and meaningful way. But, the question remains, which is more valuable to the process? There are some who believe that teaching and learning is mostly an "art" and that "science" is merely a tool; they think, "The media applied to the canvass is less important than the holistic process of creating the artwork on the easel." Conversely, others believe that the dissemination of knowledge and the teaching of skills is their primary responsibility and that "art" is not something they need to know much about; they think, "If you provide a "fool-proof" schematic, only a "dunce" would fail to understand or find meaning in the design." Nevertheless, it proves to be a spirited polemic whenever the subject is discussed.

As an example, Forrest relates a classroom strategy he uses that demonstrates the importance of both the "science" and the "art" of teaching and learning.

As a professor of educational psychology this was always the first topic I would present when introducing the content of the course. It was always a lively discussion with most of the students expressing their personal feelings and experiences about teachers they have had in the past. Some were good and some were bad experiences. But to bring into focus the fundamental difference between the two approaches I would bring a tennis ball to class and ask for a volunteer who could teach me how to catch the ball, using their best "scientific" language. Someone would always come forward and I would ask the other members of the class to help as the student tried to teach me how to catch the ball. The student would invariably begin with "hold your hands together like this, watch the ball, put your hands under the ball as I toss it to you," and so forth with specifics of what I should do to catch the ball. Finally, with the "schematic drawn perfectly" they asked if I was ready and they would toss the ball to me. As the ball was in the air I would put my hands down and turn away. The ball dropped to the floor. The students would always ask something like, "What happened?" and I would respond, "I didn't want to catch it." The whole class was so involved and focused on teaching me the knowledge and mechanics of catching the ball that they seemed almost stunned and certainly disappointed in me and my attitude of not caring or wanting to catch the ball. This demonstration served as a great segue into the importance of motivation, meaningfulness, and the "art" of teaching.

The philosophy and concomitant ideas, concepts and examples presented in *The Judicious Professor* bring together both "art" and "science" to craft a culture of mutual respect, fairness, meaning, and academic success. The philosophy propagates a fiduciary relationship of trust and care between professor and student. This is the same relationship expected of other professionals, as in the relationship between physician/patient, lawyer/client, insurer/insured, or investment advisor/investor. The ethics of a fiduciary relationship can be simply stated—professionals are always acting in the best interests of the persons they serve. In a fiduciary relationship perception is everything. It is not enough for the professor alone to believe that he or she is always acting in the students' best interests; it is the responsibility of the professor to build a relationship of mutual respect whereby every student believes their professor is always acting in his or her best interests. *The Judicious Professor* is about developing an awareness and level of consciousness, through the use of language and cognitive strategies, that enable both the professor and the student to take responsibility for establishing a meaningful teaching and learning relationship.

The authors will bring together information, conceptual understandings, and examples from five strands of knowledge that support and guide meaningful teaching and learning relationships. These areas of knowledge are professional ethics, educational psychology, effective educational practices, students' legal rights and responsibilities, and the biology of learning. We intend to weave these strands into a philosophy of what *The Judicious Professor* would, in simple terms, look like, sound like, and feel like. "Look like" would be visual impressions, "sound like" dialogical language development and listening, and "feel like" the emotional aspect of mutual respect that students and professors will experience in the relationship. This book is about language and modeling behaviors that establish and maintain a fiduciary relationship of trust and care. Will this work? Can we get there in a semester or in just one course?

Paul believes that it does work and cites his first experiences with this philosophy.

Upon return to Oregon in 1988, from fourteen years teaching in South Australia, I was playing golf with my brother when he announced he was working on the second edition of *Judicious Discipline*, a book for K-12 schools and classroom management. He asked me if I would read it and comment on the form and content. Being a doctoral student at the time, I gladly accepted the opportunity to mark up my brother's work, as my professors had done with my writing in their courses. As I read through *Judicious Discipline*, commenting in the margins, I not only found the philosophy exciting and seductive, but it also seemed to apply to the educational technology course I was teaching at the University of Oregon. So, the next term, I applied just some of the cognitive strategies to the course I had been teaching. I did not change the rigor, the content, or the course assignments; I simply changed my posture toward student achievement and learning. I altered the teaching and learning relationship. The most persuasive indication that something good had occurred appeared in my quantitative and qualitative teaching evaluations for the term. Whereas the previous terms I was getting "8 out of 10" on my quantitative course evaluations (I thought, at least I'll keep my job); I now received "10 out of 10" and students were commenting in writing about the respect I had for their learning. That got my attention and it made a believer out of me.

The proverbial "keeper of the gate of knowledge" has long been used as a metaphor characterizing a professor's responsibility to maintain standards and as a rationale for maintaining rigor and high expectations for student performance in specific disciplines. The metaphor also connotes the professor's conscience of academic responsibility to the discipline itself as well as to the greater society. *The Judicious Professor* is about the importance of student perception; whether professors appear as keepers who are only "guarding the gate" or whether they appear as interested professionals who are "helping students through the gate." We feel the professor's responsibility for "gate-keeping" should never be compromised. Rigor, quality of performance, and level of understanding must be held inviolate. Yet the manner with which professors "keep the gate" can be improved to the point that professional "gate-keeping" will dramatically enhance the discipline and further intellectual development of students. When students perceive the "gate-keeper" as one who is sharing responsibility for student academic achievement, the number of successful students will increase greatly and the knowledge-base will be widely distributed throughout society.

In all relationships, context is everything. *The Judicious Professor*, therefore, is about awareness, synthesis, and a contextualization of the cultural values spheres of art, morals, and the science of teaching and learning.

In conclusion, we believe professors must think out loud and publish their thoughts as much to learn from criticism as to contribute to the sum of wisdom. If sometimes we have made statements in an authoritative and dogmatic manner, please interpret it as our intent to provide clarity of ideas rather than from the desire to pose an axiom, or even go so far as to suggest an oracle. With that said, we sincerely hope you find this philosophy helpful in dealing with the pressures and ambiguities of teaching and learning in higher education. Enjoy the ride.

Chapter One

The Ethics of a Healthy Teaching and Learning Relationship

Being fair and consistent is extremely important to the integrity of decisions professors make, yet the ability to achieve this is made difficult because of the numbers of students and their many varying circumstances. Many of these problems are due to the constant parade of changing societal values and student lifestyles and professors reacting viscerally and capriciously to the educational and behavioral problems that confront them on a daily basis.

Most of us grew up in authoritative homes, classrooms, and schools with well-meaning parents, teachers, and professors doing what they believed to be their best under their varying circumstances. Those who were fair, firm, and used appropriate punishments gave most of us a feeling of comfort and security. All we had to do was learn to obey them. If we were caught disobeying, we could, perhaps, find something cleansing about suffering through a well-intentioned scolding, "grounding," or suspension of privileges.

When we were given responsibility in class, the "monological boss" approach is how many of us honestly believed students should be handled. An autocratic or authoritarian approach appeared preferable because problems were handled quickly and were then out of the way. In addition, most of us have succeeded in an autocratic system. "After all," we might occasionally think to ourselves, "I turned out all right." Even as adults today many still seek out the security of boundaries drawn by others.

Yet, one of the primary reasons students do not respect some professors is due to feelings of insecurity—not necessarily because of their intellectual and academic ability, but because they believe their human rights are not being respected. Empowering students through strategies that require respect and dignity and teaching students to take responsibility for learning and academic performance is not easy.

Instead of being concerned with modifying behaviors, professors should be developing and using cognitive strategies designed to change student attitudes and goals. For example, lecturing or punishing students for being late for class is only a reaction to the tardiness, but does not attend to or address the student's attitude which may have been the source of the problem. *If professors do not have a well-conceived, professional model and philosophy to use as a conceptual compass and moral guide, they are usually left using a re-active approach to academic and behavioral problems.*

A monological approach to student behavior not only creates a co-dependency, but it is a source of stress and anxiety for both parties. Professors are often concerned with what their students are feeling and thinking and students can never feel secure as to how their professors will react to their thoughts and actions. *The Judicious Professor*, on the other hand, is designed primarily to provide professors with a foundation for a dialogical, *pro-active* approach to teaching and learning. By setting in motion at the beginning of each course mutual expectations that are grounded in a philosophy that helps students to respect and learn to adhere to mutual understandings, many of the problems caused by a reactive, didactic learning environment simply do not happen.

Developing and using strategies that share power and authority with students takes time to learn and process. There are many new perceptions and expectations on the part of both students and professors that must be accommodated. All too often we expect too much too quickly. We must remember that most students come to classrooms having experienced years of "autocratic talk" and they are comfortable with being told what to do. Obedience is what most students know and understand; learning to think and act for themselves are new behaviors they need time to learn. Add to that the variables of maturation, personality development, and the fact that learning and personal growth is always gradual, and it is easy to understand why a judicious collaborative relationship takes some time to establish.

Even with these limitations and the many difficulties of shifting the class culture to a judicious mind-set, there is an appealing quality that respecting human rights and individual differences brings to the teaching and learning relationship. There is a healthy quality of life inherent in the principles of *The Judicious Professor* and this principled approach works to minimize stress and anxiety for both students and professors because of its emphasis on the individual dignity and self-worth of all students.

The ethics of teaching in higher education is shaped by a professor's perspective of his or her role in the teaching and learning relationship. If a professor believes all his or her students have an equal educational opportunity to academically succeed in class, and that it is his or her mission to employ methods and strategies to help those students learn and develop attitudes of personal responsibility, then the professor's professional ethics will reflect a *learner-centered* approach to teaching and learning. These professors are likely to respond to students in trouble situations by asking themselves questions like, "What needs to be learned?" and "What needs to be done to help this student recover?" Conversely, professors who tend to view their student's needs and interests as secondary tend to be more *content-centered*. Students experiencing difficulty in these classes are apt to hear phrases such as, "I have too many students this semester and do not have the time to answer your questions," and "I am not paid to spoon-feed you this subject matter, it is your responsibility to get this on your own."

Or stated another way, *content-centered* professors usually appear to students to be very busy with the "administration" and focus more on the "science of teaching" as they guard the omnipresent "gate of academic class standards." These professors often believe that their role is not to "hand-feed" students experiencing problems, but to teach them responsibility by leaving them to their own making. *Learner-centered* professors, on the other hand, appear to students as an educational leader who is always ready and willing to help them achieve the skills and understanding necessary to pass through the "gate." These professors rarely see themselves as "babysitters," but make every effort to view any student contact, whether positive or negative, as an opportunity to play a meaningful part in the learner's academic and personal growth and development.

For professors to become more learner-centered in their approach there must be a style and technique developed to communicate the art of judicious teaching. This art of teaching is evidenced by an ability to transcend the usual daily distractions and diversions between students and their professors through a responsible and guiding form of professional communication. If a professor's every thought and action plays off the importance of developing and maintaining the all-important student/professor relationship, the question to be asked again and again becomes; *how would a responsible learner-centered professor act upon this matter?* When style and technique are educationally sound, students will begin to sense an increased level of trust and confidence, which in turn has the effect of empowering professors with feelings of professional competence and responsibility.

The Ethics of Teaching and Learning

Ethical practices are the conscience of a helping relationship and constitute the acceptable standards of moral and proper conduct. Often ethics are referred to as "beginning where the law stops." For instance, there is no law against a professor confronting a class with "You are not as good as last year's class." But the ethics of comparing students is considered a poor educational practice, which often affects attitude, performance, and future academic success.

The foundation of educational ethics lies in professors always *acting in the best interests of their students*. Students who feel they have been humiliated and "publicly admonished" have a difficult time perceiving the professor is acting in *their* best interests. An embarrassed student seldom, if ever, can see the logic of how being put to shame and reprimanded in class is helping him or her to be a better student. Professors who say and do things that demean students often have the effect of pushing them away from the class, the course content, and a meaningful teaching and learning relationship. Instead, professors should be establishing a relationship of trust and care.

The lifeblood of an ethical teaching and learning relationship lies in all students truly believing *their* best interests are foremost in the minds and actions of the professors who are helping them to work through their difficulties and their problems.

There is often a difference between what one *says* is the ethical or moral thing to do and what one *actually does* when the issue presents itself. In defense of this difference, when an ethical dilemma actually occurs it is often complicated by time constraints, unforeseen situational factors, and emotions which are not present when one only reasons about what would and should be their moral response. Until professors are put under pressure to act, they are never really sure how they will behave.

Therefore, how one will act when the situation arises, called "*situational morality*," must be practiced over and over before students can feel secure in the knowledge of what they can expect from their professors. Experienced and practiced professors become confident that their actions and the language they use are consistent with one another. The ethics they support will mirror the actions taken with their students. Over a period of time, students will gain confidence, truly believing that their professors will always be acting in *their* best interests.

Positive Ethical Practices

Consciously or subconsciously, all professors believe in some fundamental noble principles that guide them through their daily activities. The way they were raised, the books and articles read, the seminars and workshops attended, and the day-by-day interactions with students and colleagues have shaped in each professor a personal morality concerning professional responsibilities. As these professional values develop with experience, they should serve as constant reminders of educational strategies professors should "always" be practicing. As an example, the following are a few guiding principles we have found helpful in providing a focus for our energies and priorities.

1. Encourage and model an eagerness for learning and teaching.

Just going through the motions is usually mirrored in the interest and behavior of students. Enthusiastic professors, who are "fired up" about learning activities, as well as the individual interests of students, are infectious.

Professors who are growing in their responsibilities by actively listening to and learning from their students, coming to their classes well-prepared, developing better methods of communication, and balancing their own activities with those of their students will continue to experience the rewards of good educational practice. These professors seldom tire of their responsibilities and almost never burn out; their teaching is continually being fueled by their ongoing efforts and increased awareness.

2. Model responsible professional behavior.

Students should see their professors as exemplary models of professional behavior. They should exemplify such things as following through on promises, appropriate dress and language, good organization and planning, knowledge of the subject and effective teaching strategies, good work habits, and the ability to relax and enjoy others.

On the other hand, hypocrisy and inappropriate behavior combine to undermine professional integrity and have a negative effect on the efficacy of a student/professor relationship. For example, professors who drink their favorite beverage in class while not allowing students to eat or drink are in effect saying, "My personal needs and desires are more valued in this classroom than yours." Students know immediately the difference between professional conduct and personal conduct. But professors who insist there can be two standards of personal conduct, one for them and another for students, do not understand that the real message being expressed is that professors are more valued as human beings than are students.

In the end, courtesy, dignity, and respect are community ideals professors must find ways to model if they are going to pass them on to their students.

3. Manifest appropriate personal behaviors.

Professors should avoid expressing inappropriate personal opinions and information about their private lives to students within the college or university environment. For example, whether or not a professor has ever experimented with drugs, expressions of their religious beliefs, and how they feel about certain very controversial social issues are topics that should be considered personal matters. Professors risk loss of respect, credibility, and confidence, and in some cases loss of their jobs, as the result of disclosing inappropriate information.

On the other hand, there would be nothing wrong with professors sharing with students their hobbies, activities, and interests that show they also have a personal life outside the classroom. Knowledge that their professors are human and that they enjoy an active and interesting personal life goes a long way in helping establish good communication between students and professors.

4. Focus efforts on motivation, encouragement, and building students' self-esteem.

Encouragement from professors communicates to students internal values such as courage, effort, and understanding, all of which enhance intrinsic feelings of self-worth. It depends not so much on concrete actions as it does on underlying attitudes. Tone of voice, inflection, and incidental inferences may change dramatically the significance of a statement or an action.

For example, the same words spoken to two different students may encourage one and discourage the other. Praising one student may lead to increased self-confidence and stimulate further effort, while another may think it was just an accident and not feel motivated toward other positive actions. Therefore, encouraging students requires constant observation of the effect. When praise is used to manipulate students, it is a form of external control. When it is used to give students feedback on something they have achieved, it becomes knowledge students can use to believe in themselves. Therefore, professors would be on firmer ground by replacing praise with *recognition*. By recognizing or inquiring about accomplishments, students receive positive feedback that gives them confidence that they have done something well without the pressures of success and embarrassment sometimes brought on by praise and adulation.

For example, "So what do you think about acing your test?" is much different from saying "Congratulations, I am so pleased you got an 'A' on your test." The question is much better in this case because it allows students to take control of their accomplishments and encourages them to express pleasure or apprehension about the grade. In short, *encouragement is the ability to help students look better to themselves.*

5. Accept the reality that students behave in ways they truly believe at that moment in time are in their best interests.

If consciousness automatically chooses what it deems best from moment to moment, then professors should learn to trust that all student behavior is genuine and sincere if they are to develop the mutual respect necessary for a viable mentoring relationship. For example, telling a student "If you would only try harder, I know you could do it" is actually demeaning them by not respecting their previous attempts as authentic. In the student's mind it is a "put-down" of who they were when they tried before and who they are expected to be.

Another example would be how professionals respond when students lie. The reality of a lie exists somewhere in the student's perception of the situation. Through lying, students communicate such things as fear, lack of trust, or the power of manipulation to assure getting their own way. Regardless of the reasons, professors need to look beyond words in order to find what students are really trying to communicate. An understanding response is normally very difficult, but professors must learn to accept that lying is perceived by students as a necessary action, for what could be for *them* any number of underlying and often unplanned reasons. Professors do not have to agree with students' personal logic, but they must learn to respect the many ways students will view their own reality.

6. Move toward learning goals and avoid the emphasis on performance goals.

With *learning goals* (task-involved), the issue for students is to improve and learn, regardless of the mistakes or how foolish they appear. Students who set and pursue learning goals are inclined to seek challenges and persevere when they encounter problems. With *performance goals* (ego-involved), students are concerned about how they look and how they are judged by others. Students who set and pursue performance goals often experience anxiety and are likely to avoid difficult situations and challenges as they tend to give up when they think they are going to fail. Learning strategies that build interest and meaning for students helps them to 'lose themselves' in classroom discussions, experiments, and learning activities.

For example, a Socratic approach to teaching and learning verses a straight lecture approach emphasizes learning goals that are more likely to resonate with the student and stimulate intellect in meaningful ways. When the professor and students continually pursue learning goals instead of performance goals, they tend to diminish the students' fear of performance. With students focused on learning goals in classroom activities, performance on tests usually takes care of itself. Students tend to display increased confidence as the professor's strategies emphasizing learning goals help them to internalize the new understandings and express that knowledge in a variety of ways.

7. Develop judicious rules and consequences that accept students as citizens.

Authoritative and permissive management styles can lead to power struggles, disorganization, and alienation of students. Professors who model democratic principles seldom experience power struggles because their authority is shared with students from the beginning. This pro-active approach empowers students with the principles and language of a democratic learning community and provides a classroom culture that respects all students regardless of their ability, ethnicity, culture, or socioeconomic class.

Only when students are allowed to exercise their human rights can they ever experience the responsibilities that flow from those freedoms. Through this language of mutual respect, tolerance, and cooperation, professors will create a democratic learning community in which students are entrusted with responsibility and the courage to advocate for themselves.

8. Professors should feel challenged by the problems in education and be proud they are in a position to help students.

For professors to view problems as challenges, as opposed to avoiding them, does not come easily. However, this positive mindset is essential to the success of every professional endeavor.

To illustrate with an analogy, imagine that someone is injured in an automobile accident and is rushed to the hospital emergency room for surgery. The injured person is conscious and shaken-up, and arrives at the hospital expecting to be treated by a physician who enthusiastically conveys an attitude that declares, "This is exciting work and I'm the best person to perform the examination." The confidence and interest exhibited by the emergency physician will probably make a big difference in how the patient feels about chances for a successful recovery.

It is the same with students who experience learning or behavior problems. Imagine students walking into classrooms where professors are excited and challenged by their problems, in contrast to classrooms where professors openly wish those students were in someone else's classroom. When confronted by a particularly troublesome student, how many professors would ever think to themselves, "This is going to be an exciting semester. I have not had an educational challenge like this for a long time."

As much as professors might prefer to approach problems in education with this positive attitude, this is very difficult to do day after day. But on days when professors feel challenged by student problems, they are good and they know it. However, on days when professors feel overcome by those same problems, they find themselves doing and saying things they know are inappropriate and unprofessional.

What is the answer? The answer lies in developing a "professional self," based on a fiduciary relationship of trust and care by avoiding the ego related problems of the "personal self." As professors throw their thoughts and energies into responsible teaching and administration they tend to forget about ego related issues of control and entitlement. Through study and practice comes the understanding necessary to always be acting in every student's best interests. Professors must believe in their hearts that they are better at helping students succeed than the students are at believing they are going to fail.

Teaching and Learning Practices to Avoid

As problems with students present themselves each day, it is sometimes difficult for professors to think of workable approaches or to keep from saying things they should not say when feeling "pushed to the wall." We have learned through experience that there is no one "right approach" or an immediate answer to every problem that presents itself. Each situation requires that we look at it from many sides and examine numerous alternatives before taking the most appropriate action.

What has proven helpful for us, however, is to keep in mind the things we have done in the past that were *never* successful and to eliminate those things from our teaching and learning repertoire. If you've been in education for any length of time, you know how one unthinking remark or icy stare can unravel weeks of positive interaction and reinforcement. By the expression on the student's face, you know you should not have done or said what you did, and you vow afterward never to do it again. By remembering and avoiding these unsuccessful approaches, professors not only keep intact mutual respect, but they have the time and freedom to be more creative in their search for strategies that can eventually prove successful. We have come to the conclusion that if the professor's initial actions never make matters worse, then there is an excellent chance that whatever actions the professor does take, will have a better chance of helping students recover and stay in class and succeed in higher education.

1. Never demean students.

Humiliating and embarrassing students with "put-downs" always has the effect of diminishing their self-worth. Sarcasm meant to be clever or a degrading remark flaunting power or intellect always hurts. Even teasing students about their appearance, the language they use, or ideas they express can be painful. Students need to live in a positive environment in which they feel they have emotional and cognitive respect. A positive sense of self-esteem is not something we necessarily have to give to students; more often, it is what we have to stop taking away from them.

2. Never summarily judge or lecture students on their behavior.

Instead, ask questions and listen to the student's side of the story in order to learn more about the problem. We will always view problems more clearly after hearing the other side, which makes our decision better than if we had not discussed it. As the real problems surface, empower students to make decisions and allow them to choose what *they* prefer to do. Some will decide they are ready to make a change while others may feel they need some more time or help with the matter. This learner-centered approach sends to all students a message of respect for confidentiality and a willingness to treat each person as an individual.

3. Never compare students.

All of us need to feel significant and accepted for who *we* are. Professors know there are many differences among students, but some fall into the trap of trying to compare these many differences with the hope it will work to motivate the unmotivated. This competitive approach almost always has the opposite effect, by discouraging the desired behavior. Students simply want to be judged on their own merits and not be thrust into the shadow of others.

4. Never give students constructive criticism; always give students reflective feedback.

The moment students feel they are being criticized, their thoughts are clouded by arguments defending themselves or feelings of guilt, and they seldom benefit from the constructive information. Reflective feedback, on the other hand, stimulates students' thinking and discussion directed toward the heart of the matter by keeping the "teaching and learning moment" viable. There is a considerable difference between "Let me give you some constructive criticism on your work ethic" and "Would you like some feedback on how you could improve your work ethic?" Professors who recognize the difference have found one of the important keys to helping students grow from listening to others.

5. Never demand respect or think respect must be earned; learn to give respect to your students.

By giving respect, it is usually returned many times over. Unconditional respect, not unlike unconditional love, can only be given and received. Respect that must be earned would be conditional respect. Learning to give unconditional respect is the underlying principle and basis for achieving mutual respect.

6. Never fear an apology.

If we say or do something that is wrong, a sincere apology is usually gratefully accepted and a brief explanation is genuinely appreciated. This is not easy to learn, as we often feel we are not allowed to make mistakes as professors. But eventually we learn that an apology sends a welcome message to students that they are in the presence of a sincere and honest person. Students need professors as role models who can admit and learn from their mistakes as they help students learn the art of healing and how to start over again.

7. Never accuse students of not trying or ask them to try harder; help students to try again.

Beginning a conversation with accusatory and judgmental statements about their previous efforts has the effect of making students want to try even less. Students experiencing problems want learning situations reinforced with positive educational strategies, not negative experiences that discourage them. "Have you tried this?" or "What did you think of doing it this way?" is what students need to hear. Accepting students' efforts as genuine communicates a message of confidence in their ability to learn. This may appear to be a subtle difference, but the student's reaction to encouragement will be one of renewed effort and interest.

8. Never ask misbehaving students "Why?;" ask students "What happened?" or "Would you like to talk about it?"

Asking "Why?" is like pointing a finger at students and forcing them into conversations of excuses and probably initiating an adversarial relationship. The other two responses focus on "what happened" or "it." Both are events separate from the student as a person and concentrate on situations, scenarios, and behaviors. This avoids defensiveness and tends to lead to conversations about the problem itself. Students are far more likely to open up and talk about what happened than when they feel pressured into talking about themselves and trying to explain reasons for what they have done. Students who are talking openly about the problem are students who are becoming accountable for their actions.

9. Never get into a power struggle.

The most effective way to avoid power struggles is through a person's attitude and style of sharing power from the beginning of a relationship. But if mutual respect breaks down and you sense a power play is developing, begin by taking your sail out of their wind and anchor yourself with a long tether. With your sail (ego) down, listening to students' keeps you within reasoning distance. Because power struggles are no-win situations, they can only be resolved privately through an open and honest discourse that eventually leads to mutual respect. Students will know that they are valued when the professors are willing to negotiate and share some of their authority and responsibility. Students rarely continue to defy professors they feel are on their side and are willing to listen and help them work things through.

10. Never flaunt the fact that you are the professor and they are just the students.

In most cases students usually know when they have messed up and do not need an authority figure preaching to them about their misbehavior. All they really need is a simple explanation from someone in authority who listens and gives them a chance to recover. When professors are sincerely making every effort to help them succeed as students, students will, in turn, try very hard to cooperate and help professors succeed with their responsibilities.

11. Never become defensive or lose control of your feelings.

When pride gets in the way, it has a tendency to diminish our effectiveness and leads us to do and say things we will later regret. Defensive remarks made at the height of emotional tension usually cause embarrassment for everyone. If we begin to feel defensive, we should back away and, as calmly as possible, try to focus on a resolution using words that avoid emotional overtones. If we make a mistake, we need to acknowledge our error and apologize. As a result, we usually suffer very little loss of respect, and in most cases, probably gain some.

12. Never use fear and intimidation to control students.

We find ourselves falling back on this approach when we run out of workable ideas. Intimidation works only in the short run, and its long-range effects are unpredictable and often give rise to other problems. Bitter feelings and sullen attitudes develop as students became very inventive in the circuitous ways they try to get back at professors for hurting them. We must learn to back off respectfully until we can think of a more learner-centered approach to the problem.

13. Never punish the group for the misbehavior of one of its members.

When professors hold the group accountable for the misbehavior of an individual, more often than not the wrongdoer enjoys the group punishment and the innocent students blame the professor for punishing them. Retreat as gracefully as you can if you find yourself in this box and find another way to handle the situation next time, preferably one which does not punish or interfere with the teaching and learning relationship.

14. Never act too quickly with behavioral matters.

When we "shoot from the hip" we invariably say and do things we later regret. By coming around the problem and avoiding the "direct hit" approach, errors can be corrected and the opportunity to save face is frequently the factor that turns the corner. Unless one has had good results in the past or you are certain that a direct procedure is going to work, patience, time, and plenty of discussion can be a much greater ally than impulsive responses.

15. Never say, "If I let you do that, I will have to let everyone else do it."

Always take into consideration the individual differences among students and their varying situations. Using the excuse of what others may think in response to a reasoned and appropriate decision should not affect good educational practices. Following rules and expectations is important, but exceptions to the rules can be even more important because they recognize the legitimate differences among students. Students must learn to trust that decisions regarding exceptions will be fair for all as well-reasoned decisions are made for individuals caught up in any number of diverse and often complex circumstances.

16. Never say, "You will thank me someday."

This is a poor rationale for a decision that students perceive as not making sense or having any immediate purpose. Attempting to justify what we are doing by lecturing about its future benefits or disasters has little effect on students. If responsible behavior or learning assigned course work has meaning here and now, we do not need threats to gain students' compliance. Motivational strategies and learning opportunities that address a variety of individual needs eliminate the need for lectures. The professor should want to be thanked by their students after each class, as well as some day in the future.

17. Never say, "This is easy."

These three little words, intended to motivate and encourage, instead become a monkey on the backs of students who feel insecure about their abilities. Even those who feel secure need feedback that what they are doing is something more than "easy." All students do not share our interests or have our abilities and therefore other approaches must be used in order to understand the task more from a student's viewpoint rather than our own. Being interested in and discussing the difficulties they perceive as well as their feelings of success usually has an immediate effect of bolstering student confidence.

18. Never think being consistent means treating all students alike.

Consistency in a classroom environment is providing the educational and professional specialization and skills needed to help each student believe success is possible for him or her.

Students know they have different needs and goals and deeply respect the professor who understands that one style of teaching or discipline should not be applied in the same fashion to everyone. We must listen to and observe all of our students carefully as we learn to appreciate and judiciously manage their individual differences.

Summary

The ethics of a good teaching and learning relationship are at best fragile and difficult to manage when put into practice. Initially, the professor must exhibit a general concern for ethical behavior because morality is, generally speaking, a matter of personal character. For ethics to be viable there must be a continuing, on-going moral and ethical inquiry. When professors wear well the mantle of responsibility, their biases and personalities take a secondary status to the needs of students who are guided and encouraged toward success.

Professors appear larger than life to students; as a result, they must personify a model worthy of imitation. It is imperative that professors keep alive every student's belief that they are acting in the best interests of the student, through a strong and viable helping relationship of trust and care.

Chapter Two

Learning, Motivation, and Goals

This chapter is designed to help professors understand some of the principles and concepts of learning theory. When those who work with students are empowered with some of the basics of how students learn and are motivated, it provides a basis for developing strategies that will empower students. Whether the professor is out-going or more withdrawn, strict or more easy-going, or whatever their personality characteristics might be, all can be effective in working with students if the methods used are based on sound educational practices.

The emphasis throughout this chapter will be on theory and implementing strategies that empower students with a sense of responsibility for learning and behavior. Professors who are able to shift the responsibility from themselves to their students for such things as discussions, out-of-class work, attending class on time, participating in class activities, and exhibiting appropriate classroom conduct will have found the secret of developing self-directed and capable students.

Learning Differences among Students

One important characteristic professors must possess is the ability to understand the learning differences among students with whom they have contact. One approach to teaching and learning simply does not work for all students. Therefore, some knowledge of *mind styles* can be very helpful to professors in making every class session a learning experience for all students. Although there are a number of models from which to choose, we would like to focus on Dr. Anthony Gregorc's model as an example of how professors, knowing about students' learning styles, can really make teaching and learning come alive for every student. Dr. Gregoric's Style Delineator™ was developed over a twelve-year time period. This patient and dedicated approach resulted in an instrument with remarkable test-retest reliability and face validity. Dr. Gregorc states that his research indicates that these are universal and idiosyncratic traits. All people possess all four mind styles in varying quantities and strengths. For more information you can write to Gregorc Associates, Inc., P.O. Box 351, Columbia, Connecticut 06237.

Dr. Gregorc has developed a short questionnaire that he calls a "Style Delineator." His research finds individuals on a continuum from concrete to abstract and sequential to random. From the responses to 10 questions, professors are able to categorize students into four mind styles. The mind styles are *concrete sequential, abstract sequential, abstract random,* and *concrete random.* With this information, professors are able to use strategies that focus directly on how students learn best.

Concrete Sequential

Concrete sequential students, for example, are instinctive, methodical, and deliberate in their thinking with finely tuned powers in the physical senses. They are down-to-earth and practical, and therefore like predictability and do not like surprises. These students have an urge to be creative, but professors should not look for originality in them. They are not likely to take risks but tend to seek conventionality and refinement of someone else's work. This type of thinking prefers conventionality, rituals, efficiency, effectiveness, and economy.

For these students, professors should provide a quiet, ordered, predictable, and stable learning environment. They should have professors who have a streamlined training program, functionally-dependable procedures, and a be-in-charge attitude. For them, professors must be organized, confident, and clear about their expectations and, above all, be fair, because they like to be properly recognized for following orders, doing good work, and displaying proper behavior.

Abstract Sequential

Abstract sequential learners enter into the abstract world of thoughts and mental constructs. It is a world of words, signs, and concepts that have correspondence in the concrete world. Their analytical facilities allow them to outline, correlate, critique ideas, and ponder just about everything. At times these students may appear to be absent-minded or lost in their own thoughts. Their creativity is seen through the joy of discovering new facts, thoughts, and concepts through synthesis and analytic abilities. Their creative forces extend present information so do not expect the unconventional in them. They demand incremental work that does not overstep reasonable boundaries of propriety or go beyond the material presented.

For these students, professors should provide an ordered and mentally stimulating learning environment. They should be allowed "think time" and a space for solitude. They want a challenging, stimulating classroom and, above all, time for discussions, clarifications, comparisons, the matching of wits, and debate. These students like "intellectual-types" or professors who are secure enough to monitor their self-determined learning without feeling inadequate.

Abstract Random

Abstract random students experience the beautiful, fluid world of feelings, emotion, imagination, and spirituality. These students tend to transcend time and space in order to experience the whole. They judge their experiences on their own terms and not upon the criteria set by others, which may make them appear mystical, stubborn, and self-centered. They absorb whole ideas and major themes but have difficulty recalling specific and

27

discrete details. Because of their deep sensitivity, their spirits can be high one minute and depressed the next. Their creativity mirrors human and earthly nature in all their glorious beauty. They want to express the "now" they feel inside so that human beings can learn about themselves and the world they live in.

Professors need to provide these students freedom of movement, expression of thought, and emotional experience. Subtle variations of the learning environment can profoundly affect their thinking. Variations in strategies and a helping attitude, however, can have both a positive and negative effect on their growth and development. Professors should assume the role of a guide and use their personal experiences to relate to these students. They do not like laissez faire or "anything-goes" teaching and learning styles. Because they believe in justice, they respect professors who recognize and treat students in accordance with their abilities and potentials. It is important to them that they have the sensitivity and caring inside them nurtured.

Concrete Random

Concrete random students live in a concrete world, but they are not anchored in it. These students are independent, adventurous thinkers who make intuitive leaps that often defy conventional logic systems. This ability can lead to trouble in the classroom, but they honestly cannot explain how this intuitiveness works. They need to see that something is indeed worthwhile and valid before they make any commitment. Their creativity aspect is seen through their desire to come up with ideas and inventions that are unique and original. Because of the unconventional approach they sometimes take, they are often said to be "marching to the beat of a different drum." That statement doesn't bother them because they do not mind being called "different."

Professors should provide these students with a stimulus-rich learning environment. They need many options for expression and freedom of movement as well as professors who recognize and respect their mental and physical needs. Rigid and inflexible professors stifle and depress these students. They need professors, for example, who can accept variations in the learning environment because they believe in producing in their own way and at their own speed. But most of all, they like to be recognized for their desire to move themselves and the world forward.

Professors Understanding Themselves

Just as important as identifying the way students learn is the necessity for professors to understand their own mind style. For example, professors who are random thinkers will tend to jump from one thought to another as they help students without always methodically connecting the concept neatly together. Their random students may be right with them, but their sequential students learn best when information is presented in a logical fashion and are going to miss much of what the professor is skipping over. This random approach is simply not going to be clear because to the sequential student important aspects are being left out.

By the same token, sequential professors working with random students will often get questions about something they just covered because these students are listening randomly and are only hearing part of what they are told. So when the professor gets the "we just covered that" questions, he or she should not become frustrated but patiently fill in the part of the puzzle these students missed.

Another important aspect of working with students is how the *age* and *maturity* of students affects how they learn. For example, probably a most difficult time for students is during their young adult years. These are the years students are in the middle of an identity crisis. For the first time, they are making a conscious effort to answer the pressing question: "Who am I?" They are trying to organize their drives, abilities, beliefs, and history into a consistent image of self. If students are involved in an empowering and caring educational environment during this period, then teaching and learning activities and professors can play a significant role in helping students find themselves.

But look out! As young adults attempt to establish their own identities and see themselves as separate from their childhood caregivers, they may also reject other authority figures, including professors. Professors must not take this questioning of authority personally, because it is what all young adults go through. If there are conflicts, professors should understand that students' defiant attitudes are based on experimenting with who they might want to be.

During this period, students might become disinterested in class activities. They are experimenting with many interests and activities that occasionally "crowd their schedule." Sometimes study time gets squeezed out, and as a result time to attend class becomes hard to find. Students will try to explain this "role confusion" by using all kinds of excuses. Young adults often rebel against those in authority who demand a commitment to class work or use strategies to force students to study. It is important, therefore, that professors try to avoid a judgmental attitude and develop more of a "go with the flow" approach using motivational strategies that avoid confrontational situations. This is best accomplished, as mentioned earlier, by having students take ownership for and being accountable to the class on their own terms and for fulfilling course responsibilities and taking responsibility for learning and development.

Students need professors who are flexible, patient, and understanding, and who are willing to wait for the day when a student will announce, "I have decided being a responsible student will be a part of 'who I am.' Thanks for putting up with all the crazy things I did to reach that decision." Although these will not be their exact words, the way they are enjoying teaching and learning, participating in class, and the "thank you" they voice to professors will certainly add up to meaning the same thing.

One last example of learning characteristics that could help professors understand some of the differences among their students would be some knowledge of *auditory*, *visual*, and *tactile/kinesthetic* learners. As professors begin to know their students, these learning differences will become evident and teaching and learning strategies should be readily adapted to meet each student's needs.

All of us have dominant modalities for learning. There are

only five senses students can use to acquire information (sight, touch, hearing, smell and taste). The most dominant modality for learning is visual with about 45% of the population being dominant visual learners. Next is the tactile/kinesthetic learner, consisting of about 35% of the population, and last is auditory, with about 20% of the population.

Often, frustrated professors are heard to say, "How many times do I have to *tell* you?" to students who just can't quite grasp a particular concept or idea. The answer to this question is good professors should not be *telling* students; they should be showing, demonstrating, explaining, and providing opportunities for students to rehearse the concept or idea in meaningful situations. It is important for professors to realize that students must be instructed through multiple modalities for real learning to occur.

For example, a student who is predominantly visual and kinesthetic simply will not hear what the professor has to say when teaching about course content. The professor will need to diagram the concept or idea or have the student physically rehearse and review the course content to truly make the adjustment in thinking. When professors realize that *only one in five of their students will take instruction orally*, it becomes apparent that professors had better have a plethora of instructional materials handy during class and ready for out-of-class work.

The following descriptions may help professors to recognize the characteristics of students who have specific dominant learning modalities.

Auditory Learners

Auditory learners, for example, usually appear inattentive to visual tasks. They like to talk, fiddle with things, doodle on their papers, frequently rub their eyes or complain about them, cannot remember what they just read, periodically point when reading, and their written work is usually poorly organized and messy.

For these students, professors should help them to change visual material to auditory by emphasizing *hearing* and *speaking*. The student's best sources for learning are the professor's voice, the student's own voice, or tapes, Internet and iPod casts and

CD's. Professors should always give oral directions, make sure they have the student's attention, teach students to talk through tasks, help them to use jingles or stories to aid in mastery and/or retention skills, and provide written assignments or slides that are dark, clear, and easy to read. Before leaving their class, professors should have these students talk about the concepts and ideas they are to study or even read aloud their assignment in class. Auditory learners need to speak and hear in order to learn and retain knowledge.

Visual Learners

Visual learners, on the other hand, tend to ignore verbal directions and questions. As a result, professors need to learn to be patient, as they often need to repeat instructions to these students over and over again. These students frequently daydream or have a blank expression, watch lips closely, say "huh" often, prefer to show or demonstrate than to tell or explain, get lost in rote memorization, do not remember or understand information given verbally, and often speak too loudly.

These students need visual materials because their eyes are keys to their learning. They *must look* at what they are to learn. They need assistance in changing what they hear into visual images. Professors must help these students visualize—seeing words, demonstrations, images, etc. Written assignments are very important to visual learners and will be the focal point of their organization for study. During instruction professors must not turn away from these students while talking because they need to see the mouth of the person talking.

Tactile/Kinesthetic Learners

Tactile/kinesthetic learners like to touch everything. They have a hard time sitting still and will have a tendency to move around a lot. They often write things over and over, are well coordinated, want to use concrete objects as learning aids, have difficulty learning abstract symbols, and like to take things apart and put them back together again.

32

Professors need to help these students literally *feel* what they have to learn. As a general rule, always give instructions first and then pass out equipment. Keep in-class activities short and gradually lengthen them. Vary activities with these students to offset long periods of sitting, since they learn best when active. Keep students on task during class by saying, "Tell me what we are doing here." Allow these students to move around as part of the learning experience. Activities should be divided up in short segments so students have a lot of variety in their work and learning tasks. Professors should help students plan and give them shorter sitting times. *Always try to make these students an active participant in the learning experience.*

It is apparent from the age and personality differences presented that the learning goals can be enhanced greatly when all professors possess the ability to correctly identify learning differences among students, as well as in themselves. What works well for one student probably will not work for another. In order to provide an equal educational opportunity for every student, some grounding in learning theory and learning styles is essential for all professors.

Motivation

A student's motivation can be described as the result of two main forces:

(1) the student's expectation of reaching his or her goal; and

(2) the value the student places on that goal.

When this theory is applied to a student's motivation for academic learning, they ask two questions that sound like "If I learn the course material, will I be able to graduate?" and "If I graduate, will that be valuable or reinforcing right now or sometime in the future?" If students believe the answer to either one of these questions is "no," there will be little or no motivation to attend class and learn the subject matter addressed through the course.

On the other hand, if students believe they have the ability to graduate (high expectation) and if graduating is important to them (high value), then their motivation to learn the subject matter is strong. Therefore, the intrinsic strategy to motivating students to learn is to help them believe that attending class and studying leads to academic success and that succeeding in class is of value to them. This sounds good in theory, but it begs the question "How do I apply this theory to motivate students to learn and study on their own or come to class or act appropriately in class and so forth?"

Sometimes motivation for students to learn the course content is made very easy for professors due to circumstances outside of the class. For example, a student who volunteers at a local free health clinic and is immediately reinforced, both with a sensation that they have some ability to help others with health related problems and others value that ability, will become motivated when learning about course material that enhances their ability to help others at the clinic. Now believing that studying more will give them more ability, this student will study without much need of encouragement from the professor. In fact, sometimes with these types of students, professors have to almost stay out of their way and just sit back and appreciate the student's enthusiasm for the academic subject.

Conversely, if the student's feedback from volunteering at the free health clinic is discouraging to them, the student's belief can easily be interpreted as studying does not translate into ability and that their ability to help at the clinic is not valued by others. Professors who are not aware of "put-downs" experienced by these students, or other discouraging incidents the student has experienced somewhere along the way, will have a very difficult time dealing effectively with the problem. Not knowing the cause of students' disinterest and discouragement can really be frustrating to professors doing everything they can to motivate students.

Because of the many unknown life experiences students bring to the teaching and learning relationship, it only makes sense that professors should take the necessary time to ask about the reasons behind a student's level of interest. If feedback from others is not helping students achieve these motivational goals, professors must then use more encouraging strategies in class.

In addition, professors' expectations influence greatly how students view their abilities. For example, if a professor expects a student to do well, he or she will be more patient and give more encouragement to them. But if the professor believes a student has low abilities, the student will probably mirror the expectations attributed to them by the professor. If the reflection they see seems to say, "You probably won't be able to do this," the learning goals they set for themselves are likely to suffer. Although professors cannot control the wide variations in student abilities and interests, they can provide appropriate materials and make assignments from which each student can be "expected" to achieve.

Students are also motivated to do things they feel they can do well. Therefore, professors must help students learn techniques for completing assignments well, studying for and taking tests, how to memorize important information, as well as, ways to get along with others in groups and in class. In addition, many students need to learn how to organize their day and set daily goals for themselves, and really appreciate someone who shows interest in them and will take the time to help them.

The most important aspect about motivating students is to continue to discuss with the student their goals and become an active participant in helping them reach their goals. We must avoid telling students what we think is best for them and stop expecting them to do what we think should be done. Lecturing students only turns them off and pushes them away from us and it can turn quickly into a power struggle. Educational leadership, effective motivational strategies, and plenty of discourse on the other hand, all serve to emphasize the importance of mutual respect and empowerment of students in the success of reaching their life goals.

Goals

There are two main categories of goals students can set for themselves: *performance goals* and *learning goals*. With *perfor-*

mance goals students are concerned about how they look and how others judge them. They want to "look successful" and avoid appearing inadequate. How well they performed, and not how hard they tried or what they learned, is what is important. Often students who set performance goals are likely to avoid difficult situations and challenges and to give up when they fail.

With *learning goals*, the issue for students is to improve and learn, regardless of the mistakes or how foolish they appear and students who set learning goals are inclined to seek challenges and persevere when they encounter problems.

At the heart of teaching and learning is the ability to help students focus on learning goals; instead of letting them become weighted down with the anxiety of stressful performance. This is often difficult to achieve because most students are raised with the expectations of others to do things perfectly and not to make mistakes. The pressure to perform well is one of the great inhibitors to learning.

The answer to developing confident students lies in the ability to suppress performance goals and develop in students the concept of learning goals. As a result, professors must avoid judgmental attitudes and learn to focus their language and strategies on helping students think in terms of learning goals. For example, instead of *telling* a student walking away from class "You did very well on the quiz today," *ask* the same student "What did you learn by taking the quiz today?" Telling students they do well or do poorly in academics judges their effort and ability, and has the effect of emphasizing performance goals. The pressure to perform is reinforced, so anxiety when taking tests, as well as, in class activities is made worse.

Discussing achievement instead of judging it does not mean professors should not give students feedback on their abilities. On the contrary, students need to hear "good job" and reinforcement by those who know something about their field of study. The important issue here is that the main emphasis be on learning goals, and that hearing the "good job" feedback not be perceived by students as if *they* are being judged, but that their *work* is being evaluated. In other words, students are not interpreting the "good job on your quiz" as looking good academically, but using it to build confidence that what they are doing academically is on the right track. Professors can walk this very fine line only if they understand the difference between extrinsic and intrinsic motivation.

If professors would move away from a "praise mind-set" to that of recognizing student accomplishments, it could be very helpful in walking that line. For example, "The paper you wrote was great," tends toward a praising remark. But something like, "Your paper was very well written. I really enjoyed the way you developed the main idea," not only recognizes the student's accomplishment but gives him or her feedback on certain aspects important in the assignment. If the recognition is also followed with "What did *you* think about it?" then learning goals are being further reinforced.

If the paper was written poorly with little development one might begin with, "Tell me about your main idea and what you had in mind" as a way of getting a student to recognize that there might be some problems with the paper. From there, the professor can move to helpful statements such as, "Another idea would be . . .," or "Another way of looking at it might be . . ." Educational feedback is essential to a viable teaching and learning relationships. To help students develop learning goals, *the key is talking and listening together while avoiding having the student feel he or she is being judged as right or wrong.*

As professors use these strategies, within a short period of time students will soon believe they are in the presence of a mentor who views mistakes as not something to fear, but from which to learn and grow. Students discussing their assignments, tests, and behavior are learning to evaluate themselves. Their classroom has now become a learning environment for knowledge and educational experiences instead of a place to "have to look good" and to be judged by another. The courage to be imperfect is an essential quality for students to develop as they learn to grow and develop from their academic learning experience.

Something else about student achievement that might be helpful is to understand that all students possess the *need to achieve* as well the *need to avoid failure*. This is especially important when choosing assignments for students. If a student's need to achieve in higher education is greater than his or her need to avoid failure, the overall tendency will be to take risks and try to achieve. Therefore, assigning more difficult assignments to students who are less afraid of failure and willing to master new skills and understandings will usually result in student success. They will be motivated by the challenge and will be studying long and hard to accomplish their goal of academic success. With these students, a moderate amount of failure can often enhance their desire to study and learn from their mistakes. They are determined to achieve, so they keep at it.

Conversely, if the need to avoid failure is greater, the risk will be threatening rather than challenging. Then a student's approach to assignments will be tentative. Failure-avoiding students often quit trying if they are embarrassed publicly by their mistakes. These students are usually discouraged by failure and encouraged by success.

After a short period of time, professors should be able to determine whether students have a greater need to achieve or avoid failure. Just observing their behavior, and knowing how they approach the things they do, will give clues to their motivational goals. When assignments and in-class activities are discussed and students' opinions are expressed, it is likely to be quite clear whether they would be challenged by something new or difficult, or be more comfortable by staying with something they can do successfully.

Many professors are themselves focused on the need to achieve success and often have a difficult time understanding students who need to avoid failure. Because we tend to teach best those whose needs are most like our own, it takes a concentrated effort and new strategies to be successful in helping students whose needs differ from ours. Failure-avoiding students can learn to focus on success and become confident and capable learners. But unless professors possess this knowledge of students needs, failure-avoiding students are usually pushed out of cultures that value success. In the phenomenon of becoming a good student, this is often the case.

The Brain and a Healthy Class Culture

How does the biology of knowing and learning affect the quality of the culture in which the students are immersed? From the first class to the last, a sense of others and altruistic attitudes need to be a part of that class culture. This increases the likelihood that students will keep the values and content of the class at the center of their decision-making. When students view the classroom as a safe and caring environment they will be able to take risks and take responsibility for their social action. This section is designed as a summary of the biology of learning and brain research which is more fully discussed in Appendix I at the back of the book.

A healthy class culture is based on the language of civility and operates at the principled or highest level of moral development. It empowers students to transfer a growing sense of others and altruistic thoughts and behaviors from situation to situation.

An unhealthy class culture is based on stimulus response theory, the lowest levels of moral development, and will not provide students with opportunities to transfer social skills from situation to situation, because students will tend to view each class situation as an isolated instance. In other words, there is no consistency in time, place, and manner. Every individual action is rewarded or punished by those in authority, and often what is rewarded or punished is based on idiosyncrasies of the person in authority. Students simply acquire bits of information, but are not afforded the "big picture." For example, if one professor has students sit in "special tardy seats" when they are one second late for class and another professor allows students all the time they need to make it to class, then the students will learn to do what they need to do and no more. They will not learn the intrinsic educational value of being on time and prepared for class. When professors mete out rewards and punishments and when they stem from unilateral content-centered decisions, students learn to obey the professor; students do not learn to be responsible for being prepared for class. A stimulus response culture encourages codependency and obedience. Students who view the professor's class as limiting and restrictive are less likely to take responsibility for their actions; they will simply learn to be obedient to certain authorities in a specific time, place, and manner.

A student's brain is constantly adapting to new sensory input and redefining behavior that is thought appropriate for the situation and this is reflected in the student's ever-changing ideas, beliefs, attitudes, and values. Professors need to realize and understand that students always act in ways they think are in their best interests. Students simply do the best they can with what they are physically given and with the "education" they have at the time.

Every student's thought processes and ways of knowing have microscopic origins. The ultimate unit of action, involved in all learning, is a biochemical messenger called a *neurotransmitter*. Neurotransmitters are molecular structures that relay information from one neuron in the brain to another.

One neurotransmitter involved in learning and memory is serotonin. Serotonin strengthens the synaptic connections between nerve cells involved in learning and memory by activating secondary messengers within the cell. Serotonin is absolutely essential for learning and long-term memory. Without this neurotransmitter students will learn nothing, because they will retain nothing! Serotonin is involved in all aspects of thinking and behavior. Serotonin is also involved in feelings of self-esteem and displays of pro-social behavior. One of its roles is to help individuals inhibit aggressive behavior and exhibit pro-social behavior.

Serotonin is linked to both feelings of self-worth and social behavior, and to learning and long-term memory. Experienced professors have tacitly known for years that students who have high self-esteem and tend to act in socially appropriate ways are more likely to learn and apply the knowledge, dispositions, and skills taught in the various disciplines. These students also tend to be more involved in extracurricular activities than those who feel inadequate and are denied perceptions of self-worth.

The implications for professors are clear. Serotonin is a biochemical link between behavior, cognition, and feelings of self-worth. The best thing any professor can do is to give students feelings of permanent value, and develop a class culture where students do not need to prove themselves in order to fit in with the class. This, in turn, will help to raise students' levels of serotonin, improving social interaction and learning and memory. In short, a healthy class culture is essential to developing the neuronal circuits and biochemistry needed for every student to be a healthy and viable class member.

Time and choice are essential to a healthy class culture. Time is critical to learning and memory and there is a need to provide time for "consolidation" and "reconsolidation," the physical act of storing learning in long-term memory. It takes *time* to construct the neuronal connections and transfer learning from short-term memory to long-term memory. *Time* is also an important variable in the activation of neuronal circuits or schemata. In fact, time is such a critical variable to the activation of neuronal circuits that neuroscientists measure brain cell activity in *milliseconds*.

In the brain, the coherence of perception comes out of "time" rather than "space." No one place in the brain holds meaning, rather meaning is acquired from many different parts of the brain through parallel processing of information and timely activation of schema. The faster brain cells are probably responsible for activating "stereotypical responses" that are repeatedly used over and over as responses to real and imagined stimuli. Certainly, there is little time wasted in activating these neuronal circuits as professors and students almost subconsciously play out the idiosyncratic stereotypical responses associated with social and psychological strains. For students predisposed to violence and whose environment is perceived as coercive and threatening, their stereotypical response to any problem situation or "sign stimulus" will probably be to activate some form of aggressive behavior. When these students feel little choice, their typical recourse is to act out in a hostile fashion. Generally, it is a response that they have rehearsed and imagined many times and they have it fine-tuned to achieve a desired response. However, if these students are given more *time* and opportunities to imagine different *choices*, these same students will probably learn to activate alternative ideas and behaviors as opposed to relying upon "conditioned" stereotypical responses.

Neurological *time* and *choice* are important to us all, and when time and choice are not present, problems can and will arise. Together, time and choice are great pacifiers and they are two crucial considerations professors can use to maintain a healthy class culture. *Time* and *choice* are teaching and learning resources that must be used and judiciously administered by all professors.

Chapter Three

A Constitutional Perspective

How often do you hear professors express their concern and frustration over the plethora of legal issues they are required to understand and implement in higher education today? This feeling of futility is often attributed to a national shift from the protectiveness of "in loco parentis," a legal phrase meaning the educational institution stands in the place of the parent, to the realization that students attending public institutions of higher education today do have constitutional rights on their campuses. Now that students are legally "persons" within the meaning of our nation's constitution, it is essential that professors teaching at public institutions of higher education learn both the "language of civility" and understand its application to their students. In other words, when it comes to student civil rights, public institutions of higher education are in actuality micro-cultures of the United States of America.

This point is brought home when students confront professors and administrators with a statement like, "You can't do that to me, I've got my rights." Asked to explain what they mean by their rights, most respond by saying, "I don't know, but all I know is, I've got my rights." Although many students like to use the phrase, few really understand its actual meaning.

The purpose of this chapter is to help professors learn to speak and act with self-assurance on the subject of student rights in public institutions of higher education. It provides a brief review of the historical background and the constitutional law applicable to public education. The Constitutional Perspective, therefore, functions as the legal base of a judicious teaching and learning relationship between professors and students.

The Democratic System

Students attend public institutions of higher education under a constitutional form of governance which not only provides for the needs, interests, and welfare of the majority, but bestows specific freedoms on each individual. Individual rights, however, are not guaranteed, but neither are they easily denied by the majority. Growing up in America, most of us learned that democracy is a system of government in which the majority rules. We used this to settle playground arguments by voting on what game to play or seeking some sort of an agreement on what the rules should be. Listening to children today, we realize this has not changed. Students continue to learn the concept of "the majority rules" but seldom in their educational or living environment do they learn what it means or have an opportunity to experience the freedoms and responsibilities of *individual rights*. If life in institutions of higher education is the last of their formal education, then it only follows that this may be the last opportunity for students to learn about our constitutional democracy and how students' individual rights are equally as important as the needs and interests of the majority.

The Bill Of Rights

American constitutional liberties spring from the first ten amendments, better known as the Bill of Rights. The First Amendment's use of the term "freedom" in the context of religion, speech, press, and assembly is generally considered to be one of the most important amendments to the Constitution. The clauses concerning "due process of law" and "equal protection," in the Fourteenth Amendment, are also significant and subject to widespread use and application in civil rights issues. Constitutional clauses are not self explanatory. Their meaning is translated into political, legal, and educational reality largely by the Supreme Court of the United States.

Constitutional rights exist to protect three basic values: *freedom*, *justice*, and *equality*. To live in a free society, however, does not mean we have license to do as we please. The controversy over the question of how, when, and where to limit individual *freedoms* is a never-ending issue our society constantly seeks to balance. The difficulty lies in devising a precise formula to indicate when freedom has exceeded rightful bounds.

Justice is concerned with due process and deals with basic governmental fairness. Those in America enjoy the substantive right of fair and reasonable laws governing them as well as the procedural right of adequate notice, a fair hearing, and the right to appeal the laws and decisions which take away their property and liberty. The safeguards provided by our nation's justice system are well-conceived, but as with most systems in our culture, the forces of economics, politics, and the "human factor" causes it to occasionally fail and simply is not equal to the task in every case.

Finally, *equality* presents us with the problem of distributing burdens and benefits. The proposition that "all people are created equal" has never meant that we all possess the same abilities, interests, or talents. For example, although all students may not be achieving the same or performing at the same level in higher education, it is their opportunity for the chance to succeed in public education that is their right that must be equal for all. Equality, therefore, is interpreted as meaning an *equal opportunity* for everyone to succeed. These three values—freedom, justice, and equality—have their antecedents in the United States Constitution and are basic to understanding students' civil rights.

Student Rights

Students who say "I've got my rights" are for the most part referring to the 1st, 4th, and 14th amendments. Although other amendments and legislative laws are occasionally applied to public higher education student learning and behavior issues, faculty who are knowledgeable about these three amendments have a solid foundation when discussing the subject of student rights.

The First Amendment

Congress shall make no law respecting an establishment of religion or prohibiting the free exercise thereof; or abridging the freedom of speech or of the press; or of the people peaceably to assemble, and to petition the government for a redress of grievances.

The First Amendment was designed to insure certain basic personal freedoms, which until the 1960s were seldom applied to students in American public institutions of higher education. However, in recent years numerous judicial decisions related to matters concerning free speech have been litigated. Freedom of the press has also generated considerable litigation concerning student rights to publish and distribute material on campus premises. Furthermore, the free exercise and establishment clauses in the First Amendment which relate to religion continue to have an impact on public educational programs. The right of students to assemble peaceably has been controversial on American campuses for some time, especially during the Civil Rights and Peace Movement years.

The Fourth Amendment

The right of the people to be secure in their persons, houses, papers, and effects, against unreasonable searches and seizures, shall not be violated, and no warrants shall issue, but upon probable cause, supported by oath or affirmation, and particularly describing the place to be searched, and the persons or things to be seized.

This amendment may appear to be more important to campus residence living, but it also bears upon a number of classroom situations. A student's expectancy of privacy can range from the posting of grades to a search through a backpack for suspected concealment of stolen laptop missing from the computer lab. Most faculty members do not consider themselves to have the same societal charge as that of law enforcement officers. However, effective classroom leadership requires educators to use similar guidelines when taking property from students.

The Fourteenth Amendment

All persons born or naturalized in the United States, and subject to the jurisdiction thereof, are citizens of the United States and of the State wherein they reside. No State shall make or enforce any law which shall abridge the privileges or immunities of citizens of the United States; nor shall any State deprive any person of life, liberty, or property, without due process of law; nor deny to any person within its jurisdiction the equal protection of the laws.

The last two clauses of the Fourteenth Amendment have had significant impact on public institutions of higher education. The first of these, known as the *"due process"* clause, provides the legal basis for reasonable rules and a fair and open process for denying student rights. The last clause, known as the *"equal protection"* clause, serves as the constitutional foundation for all our laws and rules prohibiting discrimination. This clause is broadly interpreted in cases dealing with all forms of discrimination including sex, race, national origin, handicaps, marital status, age, and religion, and assures an equal educational opportunity for all students. In short, the Fourteenth Amendment acts as the fulcrum; allowing our somewhat fragile constitutional form of government to balance the welfare of the majority with the countless needs and desires of individuals in our culturally rich and diverse society. Professors who understand and are able to apply the concepts of due process are usually perceived as possessing a sense of fairness and compassion when working with student problems. Because of its importance, the next several pages have been devoted to expand on the meaning of due process.

Due Process

> ....*nor shall any State deprive any person of life, liberty or property, without due process of law;....*

Picture the blindfolded woman symbolizing justice standing strong and confident, adorning the thresholds of our country's courthouses, her outstretched arm holding the familiar scales of justice. Imagine one scale heaped to the brim with all the students in higher education engaged in their studies and activities. On the other side of the scale, picture one lone student standing with textbooks and lap top computer in hand, gazing apprehensively at all of the students amassed on the other side. This graphic illustration symbolizes balancing the interests of one student with those of the majority and is the essence of "due process" as applied to public education.

In its simplest terms, due process is a legal effort to balance individual rights with the need to protect the welfare and interests of society. Only when the state is able to show a compelling reason why public welfare should weigh more than individual rights will the court's scale of justice swing toward the interests of the majority. Conversely, if the government cannot demonstrate a *compelling state interest*, then the rights of a single student will weigh more heavily than all who crowd the other side of the scale. As the scales of justice tip in favor of the individual, a judicious professor would make every effort to help the majority learn tolerance, respect, and consideration for the feelings and individual human rights of each person.

Although written succinctly, the Due Process Clause represents two hundred years of legislation and court decisions clarifying and interpreting its meaning. To fully understand and appreciate the complexity of these constitutional principles, it is important we take time to examine the clause a few words at a time.

"*...nor shall any State*" means that in order to have a right to due process there must be state action. When applied to education, only students and faculty in *public* institutions of higher education enjoy due process rights; their counterparts in our nation's private institutions do not have due process rights. The legal rights of students and professors in the private sector are expressly set out in the contract between students and the corporation which administers the institution of higher education. Speaking in legal terms, students who are dismissed from private colleges would therefore be considered guilty of breaching their part of the contract between them and the institution. The logic of the law implies that students who disobey or are not satisfied with the rules of a private college are admittedly free to choose another. Conversely, public funding of state institutions creates the state action necessary for students' rights to due process in public colleges and universities.

"...*deprive any person*" means withholding these due process rights from anyone who is legally a person within the meaning of the Constitution. For example, the law includes non-citizens as well as those who are in the United States illegally. This is not to say that illegal aliens have a right to live here, but they do have the right to due process while living here, including the right to legal proceedings which may lead to their deportation. "Any person" is broadly interpreted by the courts and today includes all students in our public colleges and universities.

"...*of life, liberty, or property*" defines those rights which may be deprived through due process by governmental action. It is interesting to note that the framers of our Constitution used just three words to protect our past, present, future, and even death at the hands of the government. For example, the word "*property*" includes everything a person legally owns and has acquired up to the present. It covers such tangible properties as real estate, personal property, and money, as well as intangibles like contracts of employment, eligibility and entitlement to welfare payments, and the civil rights of students who attend public colleges and universities.

The second word "*liberty*" begins with the present and embodies all future acquisitions and aspirations.

...it denotes not merely freedom from bodily restraint but also the right of the individual to contract, to engage in any of the common occupations of life, to acquire useful knowledge, to marry, establish a home and bring up

49

children, to worship God according to the dictates of his own conscience, and generally to enjoy those privileges long recognized...as essential to the orderly pursuit of happiness by free men. Meyer v. Nebraska 262 US 390, 399 (1923).

Too often the liberty issue is overlooked for the more understood and simpler applied property aspect. Professors devoted to helping students succeed, and who sincerely care about their future opportunities, exemplify the importance of liberty within the meaning and spirit of constitutional rights and as a result, often enjoy a special place as a role model and mentor to their students.

Finally, the word *"life"* refers to the loss of personal life at the hands of the government, such as the execution of a criminal. Due process stated in positive terms, the government may deprive a person of life, liberty, or property only after an individual has been provided due process.

"...without due process of law" means the process which is due persons by the local, state, and federal governments. Clarifying its application to everyday situations, court decisions have separated "due process" into two distinct aspects: *substantive* and *procedural.*

"Substantive" due process pertains to the legislation, the rule, or the law itself, and means a basic fairness in the substance of the decision. If the state attempted to deprive a person of life, liberty, or property, substantive due process would require a valid objective and means that are reasonably calculated to achieve the objective. The rule should:

1. Have some rational need for its adoption,

2. Be as good in meeting the need as any alternative that reasonable people would have developed,

3. Be supported by relevant and substantial evidence and findings of fact.

Whenever someone questions or seeks clarification of a rule or decision, that individual would be legally exercising his or her

14th Amendment *substantive* due process rights. In other words, substantive due process means that laws and decisions must be legal before our government can legally deprive someone of life, liberty, or property. For instance, in a classroom situation all the rules and course requirements in the course syllabus would be within the meaning of the substantive aspect. If something in the course syllabus is not fair or equitable the professor would be violating students' substantive due process rights.

"Procedural" due process relates to the decision-making process used when determining whether a rule or law has been violated. Basic fairness in adjudication is required and has been interpreted by the courts to include the following:

1. Adequate notice.

2. A fair and impartial hearing.

3. The right to appeal the decision.

Adequate notice includes such procedures as charges, evidence to be used against the person charged, a reasonable amount of time to prepare a defense, the time and place of the hearing, and adequacy of form (oral and written). When beginning a new course, this would also provide reason for professors to adequately prepare and discuss their syllabus in class.

A fair and impartial hearing encompasses elements such as a meaningful opportunity to be heard, state a position, and present witnesses. It also may include the right to counsel, presentation and cross-examination of witnesses, and review written reports in advance of the hearing. For a professor it could be as simple as listening to a student who was late to class.

The right of appeal is not only applicable to our state and federal court system, but is an integral part of our governmental structure as students exhaust their administrative remedies by appealing rules and decisions made by higher education personnel. Applied to a classroom example, it could be anything from a student appealing to the Dean about a poor grade to removing someone from the program.

With few exceptions, the Due Process Clause allows all

administrative interpretations and decisions, as well as the rule in question, to be appealed through an institution's administrative structure. From the institution, the decision or rule may be appealed to a higher state or federal administrative agency and then referred to an appropriate court. Every rule or decision made in a public institution is subject to review by another person, board, or court. A professor or administrator who says, "This decision cannot be appealed," is either bluffing or does not know the law. Many are unaware students have this right of appeal and that it is possible for their decision or rule to someday reach the United States Supreme Court. Due process, as is the case with many legal concepts, resists a simple dictionary definition and tends to be a dynamic rather than a static concept.

Other Amendments

Although the 1st, 4th and 14th Amendments are most often cited, some familiarity with the 5th, 8th, 9th, and 10th Amendments could be helpful. The self-incrimination clause of the *5th Amendment* is only applicable in questions of criminal activity and therefore not relevant in public higher education matters between students and professors where the legal relationship is in civil law. The *8th Amendment* prohibits excessive bail and fines and protects citizens from cruel and unusual punishment. While this amendment has appeared more often in suits challenging the treatment of prisoners or other persons involuntarily institutionalized, it has not been applied to situations involving students in higher education.

The *9th Amendment* stipulates that the rights enumerated in the United States Constitution shall not be construed to deny or disparage other rights retained by the people. This amendment supports other freedom arguments and has appeared in educational litigation dealing with the assertion of rights to personal privacy by students. It has also been successfully interwoven with other amendments that provide for our basic personal freedoms.

The *10th Amendment*, often referred to as the reserved-powers clause states: "The powers not delegated to the United States by the Constitution, nor prohibited by it to the States, are reserved to the States respectively, of the people." The United States Constitution does not provide a legal base for public education in America. Hence, this amendment has been the underpinning for any state assuming the primary responsibility for public higher education. Our Federal Constitution, however, is the source of all of our nation's laws and generally supersedes state law wherever there is a direct conflict between Federal and State governments.

A Pocket-Sized History
of College Rules and Practices

Until 1961, court decisions historically supported the concept of *in loco parentis*, which granted to institutions of higher education the same legal authority over students as that of a parent. In the absence of "state action," implicit in the 14th Amendment, children who live with parents or legal guardians enjoy no constitutional rights. For example, parents searching their daughter's bedroom without a search warrant, would not violate her 4th Amendment rights from unreasonable search or seizure, or a son denied use of the family car for the evening would have no Due Process rights to appeal his parent's decision. The legal concept of in loco parentis, therefore, allowed institutions of higher education the same ultimate authority as a student's parent. The only exceptions were college and university rules and decisions which were found by courts to be unreasonable, capricious, arbitrary, malicious, or made in bad faith. The courts generally agreed that higher education authorities were more knowledgeable about matters of student development and discipline than were judges and juries.

Today the law is much different. Courts rarely use the concept *in loco parentis* when writing opinions on student issues. This legal concept has been replaced by language which addresses the constitutional rights and responsibilities of students. The *Dixon v. Alabama State Board of Education*, 294 F.2nd 150, case in 1961 was the first significant United States court decision in which students successfully challenged institutional authority. This landmark case involved the arbitrary and summary dismissal of students who participated in an off-campus lunch counter "sit-in" and other civil rights activities which allegedly disrupted campus life. The students were not given notice or a hearing and were advised of their dismissals by letter. The issue was whether 14th Amendment "due process" required notice and an opportunity to be heard before students at a tax supported college could be dismissed for misconduct. The court stated in part:

> ...It must be conceded, as was held by the district court, that power [of the government] is not unlimited and cannot be arbitrarily exercised. Admittedly, there must be some reasonable and constitutional ground for expulsion or the courts would have a duty to require reinstatement. The possibility of arbitrary action is not excluded by the existence of reasonable regulations.

Eight years later, in 1969, the United States Supreme Court in *Tinker v. Des Moines Independent School District*, 393 U.S. 503, for the first time held that students in public elementary and secondary schools have constitutional rights in the area of student discipline. The case, cited ritualistically by school authorities as well as student plaintiffs, establishes general guidelines applicable to many school situations. This case involved high school students suspended by their principal for wearing black arm bands to school protesting the United States' involvement in Vietnam. The students won the right to express their political beliefs when the supreme court stated for the first time:

> ...First Amendment rights, applied in light of the special characteristics of the school environment, are available to teachers and students. It can hardly be argued that either students or teachers shed their constitutional rights to freedom of speech or expression at the schoolhouse gate...

It is apparent that times have changed from the days when arbitrary college and university rules resembled those used in most families. Today, the rules higher education authorities use must recognize and take into consideration the constitutional rights of students. If, in fact, students do not shed their constitutional rights at the gate, a graphic illustration of the students' rights might be to imagine college students dressing each morning in attire selected from their wardrobe of liberties. By the time they have donned their mail of "freedom," buckled on a sword of "justice," and grasped the shield of "equality," they might be reminiscent of knights of King Arthur's Round Table in full battle dress, as they walk the hallways of our higher education classroom buildings. This could be seen as a formidable image and possibly intimidating to many professors who come face to face with student rights issues every day.

To complicate matters even more, professors and administrators frustrated by the thought of student rights are likely to think to themselves, "The students seem to have more rights than I have." This, in fact, happens to be true. Professors have no constitutional rights in their student/professor relationship. Professors have the legal responsibility of respecting and ensuring student rights, but they do not enjoy the same rights from their students. The constitutional rights professors do have are those which flow between them and the college or university administration. In other words, professor rights come down to them from the employer/employee relationship, not up to them from the student/professor relationship. Professors must begin thinking in terms of their students as having the "rights," and of themselves as having the legal and professional "responsibility" to ensure those rights.

We are now at the core, the very heart and soul of the question facing professors today. *Is there a way to establish and maintain an effective teaching and learning relationship, while at the same time respecting student rights of freedom, justice, and equality?*

The answer, of course, is yes, and it all has to do with the judicious balancing of students' rights and society's welfare interests. Although in America we live in a free, democratic society, that does not mean we have no responsibilities toward others. Authority for denying civil rights comes from Article I, Section 8 of the Constitution and reads in part,

> . . . *The Congress shall have Power To . . . provide for the*

common Defense and general Welfare of the United States; ...

This "general welfare clause" acts as the legal foundation for legislative bodies to enact laws representing the welfare needs and interests of the majority.

As threatening as recognizing and respecting student's constitutional rights appear at first blush, there is another very important side to the scale of justice. There are, in fact, four sagacious and time-tested public interest arguments crafted in the courts and construed for the precise purpose of limiting constitutionally protected freedoms. These arguments are as genuine and well-grounded in legal principle and history as the line of reasoning which allows for individual rights. This legal principle is commonly referred to as a *"compelling state interest"* and simply means that in some conflicts between an individual and society the welfare and interests of the majority will weigh greater than those of the individual— any individual. One of the distinguishing characteristics of *The Judicious Professor* is that it helps students and faculty understand and appreciate society's desideratum and its applicability to public higher education environs.

Compelling State Interest

Prior to the 1960s, when a professor was asked by a student to explain the reason for a rule, the response could have been something like: "Because I am your professor and this is the way we do it here," or "You will have to learn to follow rules someday so you might as well learn to follow mine." The response was usually arbitrary and known as rules for rules' sake—much like a parent's response to the same question at home. A student today, however, questioning the reason for a rule should hear a response like, "Let me tell you about our compelling state interest for the rule." Although the rule may be the same in both situations, today the language and administrative posture has changed substantially in order to respect a student's right to know and question the reasons for rules and decisions.

The legality of a professor's rules and class expectations are generally presumed, and the burden of proof rests on complaining students. However, if a rule actually infringes on a fundamental constitutional right, the burden of proof usually shifts to the higher education institution to demonstrate a compelling state need. The closer rules and regulations come to encroaching on student substantive rights, the greater the need for justification and clarification by higher education authorities. Therefore, rules and class expectations which deprive students of substantive or procedural due process rights must be directly related to the welfare of the institution of higher education. For example, the need to maintain a proper learning environment is a compelling state interest which allows professors and higher education administrators to legally prohibit excessive noise during class hours or other similar conduct detrimental to these ends.

Now that it is clear professors must have a compelling state interest to sustain their rules and decisions, this begs the question: *What are these compelling state interests?* For years our nation's courts have been using four basic arguments in an effort to sustain the balance between the individual and the state's interest in our public tertiary institutions. These compelling state interests are:

1. Property loss or damage

2. Legitimate educational purpose

3. Health and safety

4. Serious disruption of the educational environment

Professor's rules and decisions based on these four arguments will, in all probability, withstand the test of today's court rulings despite the fact that they may deny students their individual rights. Educators not only have a legal right to deny student constitutional rights, but it is their professional responsibility to require or prohibit student behaviors when the exercise of those rights seriously affects the welfare of the college or university. This governmental control of student rights is generally accomplished by controlling the reasonable *time*, *place*, and *manner* of student activities. For example, colleges and universities cannot ban student expression about controversial political issues on campus, but they can insist on a reasonable time, place, and manner for its dissemination. As an employee of the state, it is clearly the professor's duty to maintain a safe and proper educational environment.

Property Loss or Damage

Care and protection of personal and college or university property is usually easy for students to accept and few are likely to argue their right to damage community facilities or take the property of others. However, during their higher education years students have many opportunities to remove or perhaps damage state-owned property as well as personal belongings of others. Taxpayers, therefore, rely heavily on the sound judgment of higher education personnel to oversee the care and maintenance of public property entrusted to them. Further, students also depend on professors and administrators to assist in protecting their property while within the jurisdiction of institutional authority. Rules protecting property should be explicit, fair, and reasonably related to the loss or damage intended to be prevented in order to insure adequate notice and proper protection.

Legitimate Educational Purpose

Professors and administrators are considered the experts in matters of academic achievement as well as acceptable campus behavior. Courts are reluctant to second-guess educational or behavioral decisions which are based on sound professional judgment. Generally speaking, all policies and decisions having a tenable educational motive related to appropriate classroom activities come within the intent of this standard. Course requirements, content, rigor, and level of achievement are examples which apply as well as certain expected behavioral standards expected in professional practicum courses. Of the four compelling state interests, rules and decisions based on professional judgment appear to students as being fairly arbitrary due to the fact they are seldom privy to the knowledge-base and context of the educational purposes for the decision. Therefore, time and effort must be taken to help students know and process the reasons behind "professional judgment calls."

Legitimate educational purpose only applies to educational institutions such as colleges or universities. However, when students find themselves under another authority, an employer for example, legitimate educational purpose changes to legitimate employer purpose or, when dealing with law enforcement issues, it becomes legitimate police purpose. This might be a reasonable analogy to use when students question what may appear to be a professor's arbitrary rules, or course expectations, and decisions which are based on this compelling state interest.

Threat to Health and Safety

A fundamental purpose of government is to protect the health (physical, mental, and emotional) and welfare of its citizens and, especially, students who assume they are in the protective environment of the public college or university they attend. Courts consistently sustain rules and decisions designed to maintain the health and safety of the majority and are quick to deny individual freedoms when they threaten in such matters. The importance of rules for health and safety are especially apparent in higher education laboratories, shops, and athletic facilities.

In addition, colleges and universities must guard against exposing students to the dangers of assaults from outsiders, improperly maintained premises, and poor supervision, as well as such things as verbal harassment and other matters which affect student's emotional health. Although students may complain occasionally about health and safety rules, higher education authorities must take steps to deny jeopardous student behavior in order to ensure the welfare of themselves and others. If student rights are on a collision course with the likelihood of harassment or physical injury, the decision must be to protect the interests of the community. Rules concerned with students' health and safety must be all inclusive, conspicuous, and rigorously enforced.

Serious Disruption of the Educational Process

The establishment and enforcement of rules that foster and encourage a proper learning environment are necessary to the efficient and successful operation of every institution of higher education. Higher Education officials have both the legal authority and the professional responsibility to deny student rights which seriously disrupt the learning process. Each situation must be decided on its own merits and may vary from one classroom to another in the same department.

Reasonable Time, Place, and Manner

In a democracy, constitutional rights can be limited by government to a *reasonable time, place,* and *manner.* These three principles comprise the standard and are the points in question courts apply when judging the reasonableness of a person's behavior. These principles are excellent guidelines and work well in democratic classrooms as students learn responsibility.

For example, students need to know that the responsibility balanced with their right of free speech can be reasonably regulated by their professors to the learning environment needs of the classroom. By using these principles, a professor could then ask two students disrupting class by talking loudly to each other, "Is this a reasonable time for this conversation?" or "Can you think of a better place to talk?" or "Can you think of another way to communicate with each other?" The questions focus the principle issues and reasonable behavior away from the possibility of a power struggle with a demand of "stop the talking." By using this approach, students are also learning to think for themselves about how to define responsibility and thereby avoiding the emotional responses brought on by authority figures telling students what to do.

When we first wrote about the importance of reasonable time, place, and manner as one of our nation's legal standards for limiting rights, we had no idea how effective it would become as a set of legal principles that students could use to understand the meaning of responsible behavior. As we have traveled around the country, we have had the opportunity to get feedback from students and educators about how they are using these ideas. They tell us they like time, place, and manner because it gives them a way to think for themselves about what it means to be responsible before they do or say something. As professors begin asking questions about these three principles, students will begin using the same language to think for themselves. The students will feel empowered with the new language. It is always reassuring to hear students referring to the same legal principles as guidelines for being accountable as our courts use to determine the legal exercise of individual rights.

Summary

Students must understand that their rights do not allow them to do as they please. Rights are quickly denied when individual actions infringe on the property and well-being of others. On the other hand, there is a professional responsibility on the part of professors to carefully weigh student human rights as they bring about the educational and behavioral expectations envisioned by the public. The best way to balance these rights with society's welfare interests is to help students think and act in a reasonable time, place, and manner as they learn how to legally exercise their rights. This is not easily accomplished. Balancing the obligation to provide for the liberties of a single student with the pressures brought about by the clamor of the majority can add up to a lot of heat in the "old college kitchen." Because of the thin line professors must tread, there may well be a need to view rules, course expectations, and decisions from a constitutional perspective in order to provide a well-regulated and orderly climate for instruction in the classroom.

The advantage to having rules and course expectations that are founded on principles of democracy means that professors *do not personally identify with them*. When personal biases are used as the basis for rules and decisions, professors are more likely to feel personally responsible and become defensive, thereby causing an escalation of personality conflicts which have no relevance to the students' education. A democratic perspective, however, allows professors to remain objective, analogous to a third party whose role it is to shepherd the relationship between the student and society's expectations. Two hundred plus years of integrated wisdom and legal authority properly presented and discussed can work wonders for professors seeking to bring about an academic semester of mutual respect and academic achievement.

Chapter Four

Establishing Mutual Goals and Expectations

The process of setting attainable goals is linked to intrinsic motivation. Therefore, it is important that students set goals and it is equally important for professors to exercise leadership by *suggesting goals students might consider*. Professors who communicate up front their expectations regarding the course and academic achievement, and adhere to those expectations, do much to provide for mutual trust and respect that can last the duration of the semester. Presenting these expectations in terms that are understandable and meaningful to students is paramount for effective communication and the establishment of a viable teaching and learning relationship.

The first class session should begin by establishing a *judicious teaching and learning relationship*. This always begins with a warm greeting with words and gestures conveying feelings of openness and trust. Welcome students at the doorway or step toward them as you first see them. *Talk a little about yourself*—all the while appearing assured and relaxed and in no rush to get on with things.

Encourage students to talk about themselves. Ideas for topics that they might share include comments about their family, associations, personal pursuits and interests, their major area of study, the various sports they play, technological tools they use, foods they enjoy, and something about why they are in the class and what they expect they will be doing in the course. Some students will have a lot to say and may talk on and on and others will talk very little. Either way, professors must take the time to listen carefully to the students' interests both inside and outside the classroom. Talking with students about their interests gives them a feeling of significance and some power in a trust relationship that is taking shape.

Depending upon the professor's relationship with the students, it is a good idea during the first meeting to discuss students' individual goals. A question such as, "What goals would you like to set for yourself in this class?" goes right to the heart of the matter. Using the words "your goals" is important at the beginning to establish a language and a focus of intrinsic responsibility. Later on, if classroom behavior digresses from the prime objective or as other factors begin to cloud the real issue of teaching and learning, the question effective professors can use to remind students of their mission will be something like, "Is what you are doing now helping you to meet the goals that you set for yourself in this class?"

For many students, this may be the first time they have been asked about their goals or have even thought about them in this context. In these situations, other questions which get students talking about themselves and the class are helpful to get them started thinking about goals. Questions like, "What experiences have you had with [this field of study]?" "What would you like to do with this class experience?" and "Who would you like to be some day?" usually get students thinking and talking about their future educational and life opportunities. As professors ask the questions and students do the talking, the words "your goals" should be scattered throughout the conversation. When students hear these words tied to their interests and future aspirations, the word "goals" has a common meaning that can be communicated throughout the teaching and learning relationship.

A student talking with his or her professor about mutual goals gives the student a first taste of responsibility in the teaching and learning relationship and some authority over what is going to happen. By employing the ideas and strategies complementary with *The Judicious Professor*, professors will be able to sustain this "student taking charge" attitude throughout the semester. In order to develop a professional demeanor, professors must begin by fighting a normal tendency to want to "control" students. Too often professors find themselves inventing an endless parade of rules, hoping to create the illusion of being in control. Many are convinced that confronting students with "drawing a line in the dirt," and the fear of punishment for crossing it, is the way to force responsibility and maintain effective classroom leadership. The problem with this approach is that once the "line" is crossed and students no longer fear the consequences, the illusion of control begins to unravel, becoming volatile at best. Until students' individual interests are respected and they begin to feel a proprietary interest in their classroom activities and expectations, a professor's effectiveness and a good learning environment will always be at risk.

Professors must learn to move away from the appearance of an authority-imposed "hard-line" method, to a more democratic/educational approach that emphasizes their skills and abilities as educational leaders. Students are far more likely to develop a conscientious attitude and become accountable for their learning when they are provided an opportunity to study and actively participate in a democratic classroom community. When they waver from judiciously imposed boundaries, they need professors nearby, not a parent substitute or a quasi law enforcement officer to pull them back into line. When a behavioral problem does occur it is an unswerving and dedicated professor who pauses to think—"What needs to be learned here?" Every student problem then becomes an educational and mentoring challenge. How much more effective our college and university classrooms could be if we would teach the rationale for society's boundaries and the values of tolerance, understanding, and the need for open-minded communication.

Establishing the Social Context

The Judicious Professor is "front-loading." It is dependent upon setting mutual expectations and goals at the beginning of class and, by definition, students need to be involved in the process. If there are no mutually agreed-upon expectations and goals, there is nothing to talk about when problems arise. Judicious professors can quickly set up mutual expectations and educational goals that are strategically revisited from time to time throughout the semester. The following procedures can work quickly to establish expectations and goals that complement the principles of *The Judicious Professor*.

✓ At the first class meeting, greet students, introduce yourself and allow students to introduce themselves or each other. Provide students with an overview of the course and your teaching and learning style. Establish the purpose of the class and students' participation in class activities. This provides students with some idea about the goals for their participation (legitimate educational purpose) and a conceptual map of what will be accomplished by the end of the semester. Then, explain to the students that you are going to ask them three open-ended questions regarding expectations of the professor, themselves, and the course of instruction.

✓ In your own words ask the students, "Given our educational purpose, what do you expect from me, your professor?" As they indicate what expectations they have of you, list students' responses so everyone can view them on a large sheet of paper or text them into a PowerPoint slide, and label the list *Expectations of the Professor*. As you proceed, negotiate with the students as they state their expectations. For example, some capricious students may say, "Give us all an 'A' in the class." That's when professors need to know the limits of their authority and offer supplementary language like, "You know, I can't do that, but I can be fair with you," or "I can't just give everyone an 'A' in the class because academic achievement grades are earned and awarded, but I can help everyone to earn an 'A' and be awarded an 'A' in this class." Often students will be quite happy with the alternative language offered by the professor. When the students have exhausted their expectations of the professor, offer some sign of agreement as an indication of your acceptance of the expectations placed on the professor. Figure 1, below, displays an example of student responses to *Expectations of the Professor* that were negotiated at the beginning of a university graduate course.

Figure 1.

Expectations of the Professor:
- Help you in positive, appropriate, and meaningful ways
- Be patient with you
- Challenge you
- Be flexible in terms of assignments, planning, and implementation
- Provide you with effective feedback
- Provide real world application for what we are doing in class

✓ Secondly, in your own words ask the students, "Given our educational purpose, what should you reasonably expect from yourselves and each other?" or "How are you going to act or participate as class members?" Write the students' responses, *in positive terms*, on large paper or on a second PowerPoint slide labeled *Expectations of Ourselves. It is important that the behavior examples are stated in positive terms*, so when students need reminding about the expectations they developed, the professor can avoid power struggles simply by asking, "Are you helping others in the class?" When examples are stated in negative terms the professor becomes the adversary, saying, "Don't (action verb)." Listing examples in positive language keeps the teaching and learning relationship intact and allows the professor to help the student come to terms with his or her own behavior rather than coming to terms with "the professor's expectations." The difference being, with the positive language, the student is encouraged to take responsibility for his or her own actions and shares the responsibility for enforcing the rules with all other members of the class; with the negative language, the professor and the class take responsibility for enforcing the rules and the "offender" feels little ownership in the judgment projected upon him or her by the professor and the rest of the class. Generally, when problems emerge, all students will need is the gentle reminder, "Is that safe and healthy?" or "Is that helping others?" and the offending student usually politely alters his or her behavior to comply with the mutually agreed upon expectations. Figure 2 displays an example of student responses to *Expectations of Ourselves* that were negotiated prior to the start of a university graduate course.

Figure 2.

Expectations of Ourselves:
- Come to class prepared, having read the material
- Arrive safely and as timely as possible
- Cooperate with one another
- Collaborate with each other
- Do our Personal best
- Be excited about learning
- Use the computers appropriately

✓ When asked to come up with expectations of themselves and others, chances are students will respond with, "We will come to class prepared to learn," "We will use resources appropriately," and "We will cooperate and be sensitive to the needs of the other class mates." As students develop their expectations, ask yourself, are these expectations inclusive of the four compelling state interests? i.e., issues surrounding students' health and safety, enhancing the educational mission, avoiding serious disruptions, and protecting property from loss and damage. If not, suggest other expectations in the form of leading questions, particularly for health and safety and property loss and damage. For example, you can say, "Should we pick up the books at the end of class?" or "How about coming in late to class?"

✓ When the list is complete, ask all students to agree with the expectations they have generated for themselves and others in the class. Go through the expectations one at a time and ask if students can "live with it" or if it needs to be changed. The professor may need to modify the expectations so that all students can agree with them and feel that they have had a say in the wording of each expectation. For example, the expectation, "Always be on time for class" may need to be modified to "Do your best to arrive on time for class in a safe and healthy way." This avoids the need for students to speed on the highway or take other risks with their health and safety simply to make it to class on time. *Do not go to the next question until all students have agreed to every expectation.*

✓ Finally, ask the students what they expect from the course and make a list of their expectations on large paper or on another PowerPoint slide labeled *Expectations of the Course*. Tell students this is a brainstorming session and all responses will be recorded. As students offer their expectations, write them down so all can see them. When students have exhausted their expectations of the course, hand out the course syllabus to the students and ask them to read through the goals and objectives of the course. The professor can even read the printed goals and objectives aloud and ask the students to compare them with their course expectations. When finished reading, ask the students if their expectations match with the goals and objectives printed in the course syllabus. Use this as an opportunity to establish mutual educational goals for the course. If students have identified an expectation that is not listed in the syllabus it would be beneficial for all if the professor included a session on that topic. The professor could say to the students, "Let's address that during week 6, can you all make a note in the syllabus to add that topic in there?" However, more often than not it works the other way; the syllabus goes beyond the students' expectations. At that point it is best for the professor to explain that scholars in that discipline, scholarship organizations and prospective employers generally believe that students who take this course will be exposed to these topics, too. Ask the students if they would agree to learn more about those topics. Usually, students will agree that they need to come to terms with that course content, too. So, with the students' consent, add those expectations to the *Expectations of the Course* large sheet of paper or PowerPoint slide. Figure 3, displays an example of student responses to *Expectations of the Course* that were negotiated at the beginning of a university graduate course.

Figure 3.

Expectations of the Course:
- Learn how to use graphics and sound in educational settings
- Have enough practice to be somewhat facile with it
- Something to take back to teach my students or share with my students
- Be more confident in our computer skills
- Learn about trends in the future of graphics and sound

✓ When the three lists of expectations have been completed and agreed to, the professor has in her or his possession a social contract articulating mutual expectations and goals, which must be disseminated to the students. The professor needs to either display the large paper lists of expectations in prominent places where all can see them or disseminate the PowerPoint slides to students via print, email or link them in their web-based course management system. It is important that all students agree with the mutual expectations as written and displayed and that they "have notice."

✓ During the semester, should any problems arise, the professor simply needs to quietly remind students of the expecta-

70

tions they set for themselves. Such a reminder should be *done quietly and in such a manner that the student is not embarrassed*. For example, when a student enters class in a disruptive manner, the professor can quickly stop any escalation of such behavior by quietly approaching the student and whispering, "How are you doing with the expectation about considering the needs of other class members?" Often this is the only thing that needs to be done. The professor will find that the student is usually quick to apologize and move on quietly.

✓ At strategic times during the semester, it's a good idea for the professor to lead students in an assessment of the expectations. Begin by asking students to evaluate your performance as professor. Display the *Expectations of the Professor* list and ask, "How am I doing with the Professor's Responsibilities?" and gesture to the chart on the wall or the PowerPoint slide. Read through the list and invite students to comment. Listen to the student feedback. This is often very empowering for both the professor and the student, as the students feel they have a valued role to play in establishing and maintaining the class environment, and the professor gets positive feedback on how he or she has maintained his or her ethical standards of educational leadership. When the students have finished giving the professor feedback on the "Professor's Responsibilities," ask, "Do we need to add to the list, or is there something we should remove from it?" This act of adding to the list or removing from the list shows students that the principle of "Professor Responsibility" remains, but how it is defined can change as the teaching and learning relationship matures. After making amendments to the list, ask, "Is there one of these that I should be working on more than the others?" Now, the professor is modeling goal setting for the students. If students will not name one that the professor should work on, then she or he should propose one of the expectations as a goal to improve upon before the next time mutual expectations are addressed in class. Then, display the *Expectations of Ourselves and Others* list and ask

"How are you doing on your responsibilities?" Allow students to self-evaluate. *It is important that the professor does not judge the students.* Allow them to do their own evaluation. As soon as the professor makes a value judgment the responsibilities no longer belong to the students, they belong to the professor. In fact, it may be adequate to simply have the students read through the list to themselves and use self-talk to assess their adherence to the mutual expectations. When the students have finished their self-evaluation, ask, "Do we need to add to this list, or is there something we should remove from it?" For example, students may suggest that they no longer need the statement, "Cooperate with each other," because they already do that very well and they really do not need to have that in writing. They might argue that expectation simply does not need to be up there. If all students agree, then the professor can remove that expectation from the list. Adding and removing expectations from the list illustrates how the principle persists, i.e., students have responsibilities to each other, and their expectations can change, within principle, as their working relationships mature over time. After making amendments to the list, ask the students "Which of these Student Responsibilities would you like to work on?" Have the students set a goal for themselves, as modeled by the professor previously when addressing the *Expectations of the Professor*. Finally, ask about the *Expectations of the Course*. The professor may indicate, we're five weeks into the course or about a third of the way through, do you think we've addressed the course expectations to that degree? Ask if they would like to add to the expectations of the course, or if things are falling behind negotiate with the students as to what is most important for them to learn.

✓ After reviewing the mutual expectations and goals, display them for all to view or provide another copy for every student. When professors embrace the use of and develop mutual expectations and goals with their students everyone is working toward the same ends and it is never too late to "start over again" and work to make things better for all concerned.

The simple beauty in these procedures is that students *set their own goals* and *determine whether or not the goals were met*. The professor never "owns" their expectations, but helps to develop the expectations within the guidelines of the four compelling state interests, reminds students of their commitment to the expectations, and helps to realign non-compliant behavior with the social expectations set by the class. The professor always remains on the "student's side."

Sometimes a student will try to put the professor in an adversarial role. Should this happen, simply say, "I'm on your side on this one." Often this simple statement quickly deflates a volatile situation. The student simply needs to be reminded that *the professor does not own the expectations* and that she or he is trying to help the student come to terms with mutually agreed upon expectations when behavioral problems occur.

Following these procedures does much to avoid power struggles and ensures that the responsibility for maintaining a respectful class environment rests squarely on the shoulders of every individual student.

Continuing the Dialogue

Professors help students acquire a real sense of belonging through the use of *dialogue* about issues pertinent to the class culture. As well, dialogue provides opportunities for professors to model respect and trust by actively listening to and valuing students' ideas. By discussing the class culture and teaching and learning goals, the professor has set in motion an essential part of the effective operation of all judicious teaching and learning relationships.

Professors can invite dialogue regularly at the beginning of each class. Such class discussions work to share power; and as a result, do much to *avoid power struggles* by providing every student with an opportunity to ask questions and express concerns and delights. When students feel they have some power in the organization and operation of their learning and class environment, they are less likely to "act out." *Invitations to dialogue* provide "institutionally okay" ways for students to vent their frustrations, anxieties, and to celebrate in a fair and equitable manner. When students know that they have some stake in the action and that they were an important part of the decision-making process, *students are more likely to participate as a positive force in the action.*

There is no "right way" to conduct these discussions. The "best" structure for a given professor and students will probably emerge as the semester progresses. However, there are some elements that work well to facilitate and democratize the process. The list of elements that follow may be helpful in preparing students for discussions about their classroom and goals.

Determine the best time, place. and manner for dialogue.

Some professors let students know that any student can call for class discussion whenever it is needed. Other professors determine a specific time, place, and manner. For example, every class will begin with a short discussion on how we are doing with our expectations and learning goals. Both strategies can work well as long as the class discussion has the effect of giving students a sense of significance and some power and control over what happens in their learning and class environment.

The professor should lead the discussion.

The class needs an educational leader; that is the professor's responsibility. Class members should not lead the class discussion. They should be equal participants, but they should not lead the meetings. When class members lead the meetings, implicitly the class is divided and expectations are placed on the discussion leader that may be unwanted or unacceptable to other class members. Allow each student to express his or her opinions without the added responsibility of conducting the class discussion.

Set the ground rule never to use the names of people in class during the discussion.

Negotiate with students not to use peoples' names during the discussion. When the professor suggests this, most students are quick to agree that individuals would feel embarrassed and defensive to have others talking about them. Suggest that when talking about problems and behaviors that the discussion should talk in terms of, "a person who acts in this way..." rather than, "When (Person's Name) acts like..." This technique protects individuals in the class discussion and allows everyone to focus on ideas, concepts, actions and behavior; and not on personalities.

Students should never be coerced to participate in the class discussion.

It should be okay to "pass" if someone chooses not to contribute to the discussion. Coercion is antithetical to the principles of *The Judicious Professor*. Hopefully, students will feel comfortable enough to contribute to the class discussion when they feel it is in their best interests and the best interests of the class to voice their opinions. Sometimes, the best contribution individual class members can bring to the meeting is simply to be a good listener.

A good way to begin class discussions is to have students talk in small groups for a couple of minutes.

Provide guidelines or categories for students pre-discussion and display these guidelines for all to see. Using three categories is desirable, encouraging everyone to list at least one thing in each category. Always ensure that one of the three categories allows students to raise issues that are problem areas, another category enables questions, and the third category encourages celebrations and the acknowledgment of success. Some guidelines or categories that have worked well are: Concerns, Clarifications, and Delights, *or* Something I'd like to Talk About, Something I'd like to Work On, and Things that are Going Well.

After a couple of minutes, assemble as a whole class and use the concerns and clarifications as a discussion agenda.

Begin by asking, "Does anyone have concerns or clarifications they would like to discuss?" Save the "Delights" for the end of the discussion as they tend to make everyone feel good and do much to build class harmony.

Periodically, revisit the class expectations of the professor, students and the course.

After discussing concerns, clarifications, and delights, the class can revisit the expectations set for the professor, themselves and the course of study. The professor can ask, "How are we doing with the expectations we set for me, you, and the course?" Self-assessing goals and expectations in this way demonstrates how principles of civility can be maintained through a dynamic process of evaluation, negotiation, and dialog.

Limitations on Negotiating Expectations

There are legal limits to the latitude of legislative authority professors have when structuring rules and course expectations appropriate to their educational responsibilities. A professor, for example, may adopt specific rules and course expectations for their class as long as they do not violate the rules of their Department Chair, as well as all those in authority above the Chair. The rules of the college or university and the state system, in turn, cannot subtend state and federal legislative laws, state and federal case authority, or the United States Constitution. In other words, we are all subject to certain "givens"—rules that have been already decided and must be followed by all within their meaning and jurisdiction.

Faced with all the legislative and administrative strata, professors may feel at a loss trying to locate and assimilate all the pertinent laws and regulations which affect their classroom rules and decisions. As a way of bringing this into focus and getting on top of the "givens," three publications should be read and studied carefully. *First*, review the rules and regulations published by the Department. These should take into account all departmental policies regarding administrative responsibilities and student rights as they relate to the unit itself. *Second*, professors should become familiar with the rules of the College or University and the regulations applicable to teaching faculty. And *third*, know well the institution's student handbook and all the rules on campus affecting student activities and programs. Learn the boundaries and the rules you cannot change and make every effort to respect and enforce these rules. If there is disagreement with a rule or decision, discuss it directly with the person responsible for it. It's hard to say this delicately, but violating administrative rules or "the givens" is simply called *insubordination*. The often cited "academic freedom" argument, in most cases, will not legally prevail over an administrator's reasonable request.

Rules or expectations are best written in broad general terms, inclusive enough to account for all possible student behaviors. However, a rule could be unconstitutionally vague because of its breadth and, as a result, violate student's procedural due process rights to adequate notice. For instance, a general rule like "Treat all property with respect" is not specific as to what needs to be done to properly care for and protect the property. An initial broad heading should be followed by examples and preferably a discussion of expected student behavior. The examples need not be exhaustive, but should encompass a number of possibilities in order to bring about student awareness and understanding of what is expected. Examples could be from past incidents as well as any problem areas that can be reasonably anticipated.

Expectations should be kept to a minimum and be followed by appropriate examples which would be easy for students to remember and staff to manage and enforce. This two-pronged approach will address students who argue, "The rules didn't cover that," as well as students who claim, "I didn't know what you meant by the rule." The law does not require college and university authorities to anticipate in advance and state in writing all of its rules before school begins. Courts allow reasonable additions and deletions during the school year. The central question is whether the professor can show reasonable cause for the rule change and whether students are given adequate notice before compliance is enforced.

Of equal importance to the legality of classroom expectations is the message they communicate about how students will be valued. The college or university catalog, student handbook, and most importantly the course syllabus, are for most students their first impression of the management style of the professor. Rules and course expectations that generate a positive feeling of support help alleviate fears and belligerent attitudes many students have, typically brought on by anticipated encounters and past experiences with stereotyped authority figures. A good beginning would be to develop a classroom philosophy statement based on students' human rights and from which all rules and decisions will flow.

A clear philosophy statement at the beginning of a course syllabus indicating how students will be valued and respected is a powerful and definitive message. It would also be an excellent topic for class discussion during the first class session, helping to establish the professor's teaching and learning and classroom management style. As with any other philosophy statement, writing it down and discussing it with others has the effect of serving as a constant reminder about its importance in creating a compatible classroom environment.

Chapter Five

Judicious Consequences— A Professional Responsibility Model

Rules and expectations serve the purpose of providing bound-aries and are effective only until they are broken. When students waiver from judiciously imposed boundaries, they need a profes-sional educator and mentor nearby who is able to guide and support their recovery. A professional educator and mentor is someone who acts as a wise, loyal friend and advisor; one who is always acting in students' best interests, not by making them dependent, but by deepening their confidence in their abilities to devise their own solutions. When a behavior problem does occur, it is a dedicated mentor/professor who pauses to think—*"What does the student need to do now to rebuild the damage and what can be learned from what happened?"* Every student's problem then becomes an educational opportunity.

When professors direct their thoughts and efforts toward a professional responsibility approach by utilizing mentoring strat-egies as the way to resolve problems, students are not as likely to perceive themselves as being treated unreasonably. Case in point, when students make academic mistakes, good professors use these mistakes for diagnostic purposes and employ effective educational strategies to help students overcome their learning difficulties. Professors are usually patient and understanding with students and know that academic accomplishments take some time to develop. It would only follow then, that the same professional approach toward behavior problems would be equally as effective.

Judicious Consequences

When a rule is broken, professors usually begin thinking in one of two completely different directions: (1) How shall I confront this student with the infraction and what would be the most appropriate punishment? or (2) What more do I need to know about this situation and which educational and mentoring strategies will be most effective for bringing about a reasonable resolution? Each of the two perspectives conjures up various scenarios, at times mutually exclusive, and each eventually becomes the basis of new expectations as consequences are played out.

To many professors the first scenario may appear to be the more reasonable approach; the violation of rules followed by "an eye for an eye" or "pound of flesh" type of punishment would seem to represent a logical extension of the justice model. After all, isn't justice what *The Judicious Professor* is all about? Contradictory as it may seem, judicious consequences for misbehavior are exactly where the justice model must be abandoned and a completely different approach must be used—that of a *fiduciary relationship of trust and care*. It is a relationship where students are entrusted to the capable hands of professors responsible for their success in higher education.

Although the principles of justice work well in the development of fair and just rules, the justice model carried over to consequences may work as a detriment to professors seeking to change attitudes of misbehaving students. Within the criminal/justice system, for example, offenders are punished by sending them to jail, or in the case of a student in a college or university settings, pushing them out of the classroom and out of higher education. Criminalizing students' misbehavior and isolating them from others is exactly what students in trouble do not need.

Students experiencing problems are already feeling badly about themselves, and they do not need professors compounding their problems by making them feel even worse. Rather, such students need help and support to resolve their problems in ways that will increase their feelings of self-worth. The criminal/ justice system is traditionally society's last resort for resolving community problems and is used by our government only after everything else fails. Therefore, it does not make sense for professors to use the criminal/justice model first, before employing what they were professionally prepared to use—educational and mentoring approaches. Consequences then become ways for students to learn responsibility, rather than predetermined acts designed for retribution or to foster obedience.

Moving away from monological to a dialogical approach is not easy. We have found that it takes time and a lot of practice. Many professors have discovered that they are most successful in establishing a professional relationship with students in trouble when they try to visualize their situations in broader terms than what appears to be the immediate problem. The following are some mental images professors can use that help them gain a broader perspective: (1) If I am this student's educator and mentor, I had better listen and act as his or her loyal friend and advisor; and (2) I must keep in mind that this student is not finished yet, but is in the process of developing awareness; and, therefore, (3) I must decide what I can do *now* to help him or her recover and learn something from an error in judgment.

Simply stated, professors need to try to filter everything else out of their minds and make every effort to keep a focus on their responsibility as a professional. If professors begin to think about their biases, they have a tendency to judge students' misbehavior and lose their concentration on the important issues of students' success and well-being. Professors are most effective when their energy is directed toward students in a concentrated effort, sincerely trying to help them process their behavior and understand their responsibilities.

The nature of judicious consequences embodies a holistic approach and implies a resolution that balances all ramifications and possibilities. It begins with identifying issues central to students' emotional development and educational needs in order to determine the compatibility of the professor's professional practices. It involves such questions as:

1. What needs to be learned here?

2. What is my role as a mentor/professor in resolving the problem?

3. Do I need more information about the events surrounding the problem?

4. What strategies can I use to help this student to talk about the problem?

5. How will the student perceive what I am trying to do; i.e., help with recovery, punish the misbehavior, etc.?

6. How will the problem's resolution affect the other members of the higher education community?

7. *And*, in order for the important issues of the problem to unfold and for workable solutions to take form, how can I keep intact the mutual respect needed for a strong professional relationship?

A judicious style, therefore, would be exemplified as wisdom blended with authority to make decisions and act upon them, but only after pivotal questions have been considered and the real issues have emerged. The move away from "autocratic talk" to communicating respect and dignity flows logically from asking "judicious questions." Engaging students in discourse is a strategy that ultimately empowers both students and professors through the role each plays in their shared responsibility for the learning process.

Responding Professionally

If asked to re-title *The Judicious Professor*, we would call it something like, *How, When, Why, and Where to Back Off*. This is not to be confused with backing down or inaction, backing off is simply using an approach that weighs all sides of the question so that responses can be tailored to ease into the most important problems. Instead of trying to be too inventive or manipulative, professors should learn the technique of "backing off." Often, this provides the space necessary for everyone to process the incident and see it in a new light. Time also allows other forces to be brought to bear upon the matter, letting many situations simply play themselves out to a positive end.

Sometimes professors exacerbate a situation and a "me against them" mentality develops. For example, a flippant response by a professor to the verbal threats of a student, such as "Is that all you have to say for yourself?" is in essence a counter-attack by an authority figure that immediately escalates the confrontation. Whatever is said next by either party is usually the language antagonists express to each other. Rather, confrontational students need someone in authority on their side; they need to hear something like: "It sounds like you are upset. Would you like to get together and talk about it?"

Talking about the problem after some "cool down" time would not be backing down or avoiding the issue, but it is viewed as backing off, allowing students time to process what they have done as well as creating an opportunity for a private meeting. In times of trouble, students need support and need to believe that professors are really working in their best interests.

It is very important when a disruption occurs that the first reaction comes from a professional educator who is acting in the best interests of the student. This reaction is consistent with an educator's professional preparation and responsibility, and is hopefully what professors do best. The following illustration will emphasize the point.

Imagine the front of a classroom is filled with the people who impact student lives. Standing there is a professor, parent, counselor, college administrator, religious leader, a law enforcement officer, a social worker, a judge, and an employer. Now, with all of these people present, a confrontational student from the back of the classroom shouts at the professor: "You '(expletive deleted).' You gave me a 'D' on my test."

In this crowd of people witnessing this moment of public defiance, what role should the professor play? The answer is—

that of a professional educator acting in the student's best interests. If that professor is the student's best chance for academic success in that discipline, the trust and care of a professional relationship simply must be kept intact. To accomplish this, the primary task of the professor is to avoid the pitfalls of trying to assume the roles of the other people who are congregated at the front of the room.

The professor's response to the student might be something like: "Sounds like you are really upset about the test. Do you want to talk about this now or can it wait until class is over?" The message would be clear to all that the professor is sincerely interested in the welfare of the upset student, as well as, with the importance of continuing on with the class. With this kind of "recognition" response, the professor would not be backing down nor condoning the student's behavior, but exemplifying the professional demeanor and the empathy necessary to keep intact a strong teaching and learning relationship. In addition, by responding with a question, the professor allows the student to retain some power in the relationship. Just as with establishing rules, if consequences are to be effective in changing attitudes and behaviors, students must have some authority over their actions in the life of the consequences.

With practice in using this approach, professors will begin to look past rude and offensive language directed at them. Instead, each student's behavior, no matter how disruptive, will be perceived as an indication that something is wrong and the professor will respond by going *indirectly* to what needs to happen next.

In contrast, professors who abandon their role of the "professional educator" by stepping into one of the other roles actually diminish their teaching integrity and eventually their effectiveness in the teaching and learning relationship. For example, professors who attempt to parent students, preach to them about religious values, or warn them about future college or university and employment disasters, usually experience a sigh and the rolling of the eyes, flippant wisecracks, argumentative comebacks, or any number of other "turn off" mechanisms that students use to distance themselves from lecturing and judging professors.

When professors lose their students this way, students lose their professors, and students as well as professors both lose in the process. Professors are the student's best and sometimes their only chance for success in a given subject or discipline. For this reason alone, professors must avoid assuming the roles of others and keep pure a relationship that fosters a continuing rapport and confidence. Although students with problem situations often leave classrooms for a short period of time, they usually come back. When the educational relationship is kept healthy and students believe they have not lost a professor, returning students will always feel welcomed back.

Very important when developing a professional relationship is setting the stage properly. The handling of student problems usually occurs on the professor's turf. It is, therefore, important that a cordial invitation is extended to students. Professors coming around desks greeting students, as they would another adult, are showing a sign of respect. Something like "come on in—it looks like we have something to talk about" quickly establishes the importance of the students' worth and clearly invites conversation. Without a genuine invitation to conversation, trying to "develop the question" can quickly turn into a lecture.

Although professors make every effort to craft their office or classroom into an inviting place, some students are unwilling to discuss problem situations there. One approach is to meet these students at a neutral site, or even on their own "turf," much like making house calls. This more balanced playing field for discussion often relaxes students enough to let them open up and get to the real problem. Offices and classrooms can sometimes be threatening and intimidating places for students who are unsure about themselves in the higher education environment. The concept of "territory" is powerful and one that students tacitly respond to in ways that can affect their participation and open discussion about the problem situation.

Developing the Question

The first words spoken to a student experiencing problems should be in the form of a question. Questions avoid accusatory

85

statements and lectures and immediately begin the healing process by sending a powerful message that you are acting in the best interests of the student. Accusations and lectures are monological approaches and push the student away, whereas beginning with questions is a dialogical approach which empowers students with shared responsibility. The person talking not only has the power, but the responsibility for what is said and the action emanating from the discussion. In every professional relationship, the conversation always begins with asking questions of clients and they do the talking before making any decisions.

Physicians, for example, would not prescribe automatically two aspirin to every patient who complains of feeling ill. Rather, physicians respond to medical problems with: "Where does it hurt?" "How long has it been that way?" and "Is it worse when I do this?" Before a lawyer agrees to represent anyone, considerable time is taken pursuing the facts and interests of the client. Without gathering appropriate and relevant information, professionals simply cannot act in the best interests of the people they are employed to serve. Just as with other professional fields, professors must learn to approach discipline problems by asking the relevant professional questions.

Defining the Problem

Academic and behavioral problems should be approached by asking general questions of inquiry and concern in an effort to encourage students to talk about what *they* perceive happened. "Coming to the point" does not mean beginning with an accusatory statement. It means approaching the problem from the *perspective of the student* with the intent of getting to the heart of the problem. Asking "what happened?" or "Is there something I can do to help?" or offering a descriptive statement like "it looks like you might be having a bad day—would you like to talk about it?" usually prompts students to open up and discuss the problem.

The focus of the conversation must be away from students defending who they *are* to encouraging them to talk about what they have *done*. Therefore, always avoid asking students "*Why?*" questions. "*What* happened?" or "Would you like to talk about *it?*"

86

focus on a description of the situation, thereby separating students from their acts. This strategy is essential for students to feel professors are acting in their best interests. When professors appear to students to be on their side, a professional relationship develops thereby avoiding the possibility of an adversarial relationship.

Students who are in trouble usually know the rules and are aware that they have messed up. Given the opportunity to speak with a professor they trust to be working in their best interests, many students, on their own volition, will bring up the infraction and be quite willing to talk about it. Students who are talking about how they perceive their misbehavior in relation to the situation are beginning to take ownership of the problem, and, if properly handled, will eventually become accountable for their actions.

Questions have a way of "softening the blow" to someone who might be in the wrong, and allow them some space to save face and recover. It also gets professors away from sounding threatening or accusatory, which helps keep intact a mentoring relationship. For example, a professor who says "this answer is wrong" tends to create defensiveness in students. But a professor who asks "does this answer look right to you?" softens the error and immediately empowers students to take responsibility in the recovery process.

By asking "leading questions" and listening carefully, the underlying issues begin to emerge. Professionals in every field get very adept at asking leading questions based on their expertise and intuition. "Professional probing" can take many forms, such as personal reactions, interested inquiries, or even a shared opinion on the subject. For example, students caught cheating on a test do not need a lecture on morality, but rather an opening response such as: "What happened? Could it be that you did not have adequate time to prepare for the test?" and then, they need a chance to recover.

Also, during the probing period, a well-placed "Would you tell me what you have decided to do about that?" keeps the focus on just who is accountable and in charge of the resolution.

Just changing the approach from "I am in charge here" to that of mutual respect improves communications immediately. For example, "Will you be able to complete your term project before I need to turn in your grade?" might replace "You had better get busy on your term project. You know it is due by the end of the term." Another example would be, "When can we talk about your test last week?" which could replace a demanding statement like "You had better see me soon about your poor performance on last weeks' test."

Leading questions that replace stated limits and demands have the effect of showing respect for students' judgment. These leading questions, however, can include the same ideas and suggestions which are often the subject of demanding statements or lectures. By putting opinions and advice in questions, one avoids confrontations while at the same time empowering students. It is a strong message to students that they have significant control in their education as well as the responsibility of an equal partner in their success in higher education.

Students who do not respond to questions immediately, or who refuse to discuss the situation, often need more time to process their feelings. When faced with stubborn attitudes, professors should not force the conversation, but instead say something like, "I see that you would rather not discuss this now. Maybe we can get together later, when we both have had time to think about it." In many cases, students need some time to get past the hurt or embarrassment they feel before they are ready to talk.

Whether it is about misbehavior, a request for advice, or even support for something done well, professors want to say the right thing, not something that will discourage students. Experience has taught us that the "right" response is not nearly as important as having an empowering attitude. If professors are focused on *listening*, discourse leading to positive interaction tends to flow easily. With such an attitude, it seems that no matter what is said, it will be interpreted by students positively and professors will be perceived as acting in their best interests.

In summary, something as simple as a dialogical approach of leading questions and listening become a strategy that can be used over and over again with the same powerful effectiveness—

that of empowering students. As a result, the more authority students have over their learning, the more they are accountable for their own thoughts and actions; whereas a monological approach is designed to modify behavior, dialogical strategies have the effect of changing goals. For students to believe in their professors, and to look to them as loyal advisors and sagacious academics is by no means a given; it is something that must be practiced and celebrated everyday.

Shaping Consequences

Before problems arise engaging students in classroom discussions about possible future consequences is an important aspect of *The Judicious Professor*. Although judicious consequences should not be predetermined for each future misbehavior, students do have a right to know what kinds of consequences they will be discussing with their professors when it comes to minor and major infractions of the rules. Previously discussed consequences, therefore, give students and professors a kind of "ballpark figure" starting place when it comes time to sit down and work things through. If students are involved in discussing consequences to rule violations, they will not only feel a shared ownership, but are far more likely to accept their responsibility when or if the time should come.

A professor's approach to shaping consequences should reflect the basic principles of empowerment and student responsibility and avoid forcing explanations from students about what is already past. Students should know that when rules have been broken, their discussion with professors will center around two important future aspects: (1) *What needs to be done now?* and (2) *What can we learn from this?*

"What needs to be done now?" usually involves two concepts, *restitution* and an *apology*. Both are designed to restore wholeness. For example, when a student is caught taking something from another student, the leading questions center around restitution of the property and a discussion of an appropriate apology. By focusing on just two aspects intended to restore property and feelings, professors can avoid the negative effects of punishment and focus on empowering strategies to make things whole again. Students and professors too often get mired down in superficial arguments of right and wrong which are not constructive to successfully resolving the issue. While "what needs to be done now?" is meant to take care of the past, "what can we learn from this?" is directly related to the professor's commitment to changing future goals and attitudes of students. There is a significant difference between consequences designed to modify behavior and those that lead to changing goals. A professor's ability to help students view themselves differently as a result of a negative experience is truly an example of the art of teaching.

Of great importance to effective communication is that both parties believe they have some control in the conversation. While working toward an equitable solution, students must believe their feelings and opinions are a valued part of the process.

The secret to shaping consequences, therefore, is to work with students on solutions that are *volitional* on their part—a process in which they feel *they* have made the decision and that *they* "have made something right again" when it is carried out. In the long run, this sense of accountability feels much better to students than being "let off the hook" with a lecture.

A good example comes from a professor who recently told about an encounter she had with one of her students. Sitting together in her office, they had just agreed upon a solution to a problem. As the student was leaving her office, she asked, "You're not going to have any trouble carrying out your part of the bargain, are you?" The student turned to her with a look of disbelief and said, "Why would I? It's my agreement, isn't it?"

Exemplifying and modeling the intended behavior is also an effective strategy for empowering students. Professors should not hesitate to join in and help students who are having trouble. Modeling problem solving is far from a picture of vulnerability or even of indulgence; instead it is a demonstration of strength, cooperation, and leadership qualities. It also provides an excellent opportunity to do things *with* students instead of doing things *to* them.

Professors should avoid shaping consequences before behavioral problems occur. For example, a professor who threatens, "If you do that one more time I will ask you to leave the classroom" would be setting in motion a possible action from which it would be hard to retreat.

Professors who do this often box themselves into making a poor decision. Another problem with predetermined consequences is that students often play games with threatened "cut-and-dried" consequences. For example, knowing that the third absence means a grade reduction almost invites two absences from students who enjoy "pushing the envelope." When narrow lines are drawn, students seem to want to stand on them or jump back and forth over them. However, professors who are patient and confident in their professional abilities draw broad lines students must walk across. This gives them time to diagnose the problem and help students change their attitude before they reach the other side.

Individualizing Consequences

There are two important aspects in determining consequences for each student's misbehavior. The first is to understand the real nature of the problem, and the second is to account for individual differences among students.

For example, if two students who neglected to clean up last class session's lab work were asked by their professor why the experiment was not cleaned up, and one student replies "OK, thanks for reminding me I can clean it up right now and that won't happen again" but the other student belligerently responds "that's not my job, that's janitor's work and you can't make me do it." The underlying problem is different for the two students. As a result, a different approach and consequence would be needed to get to the heart of each student's individual differences. In the case of the first student, the experiment would be cleaned up willingly, and in all likelihood would not be perceived as punishment but rather as a reasonable act of recovery from someone ready to make amends and get it over with right away. As for the other student, a more serious problem has surfaced, and cleaning up after the experiment now becomes secondary to dealing with an attitude that is now apparent as the underlying problem.

This is exactly the time students need individual attention if they are going to continue in class. It is also precisely the moment a professor needs to keep personal feelings of anger and frustration under control. The use of effective communication and problem solving skills become the important next steps as the true nature of the difficulty presents itself. Workable resolutions will emerge as students temper their anger and have an opportunity to express their side of the story in the problem solving process.

This mutual process of working towards a resolution often requires time for student attitudes to change. When this change does happen it may be too late for the second student to help clean up the experiment. But with a change in attitude, it is likely the second student could decide to rectify his or her past indiscretion by participating in clean-up activities in the building as well as apologizing and thanking those who did clean it up.

On the other hand, if both students felt they were forced to clean up the experiment, the first student who did not need to be coerced could resent it as punishment, and the second student's indignant attitude would not only go unattended, but could lead to bitter reprisal and an escalation of the problem. This is the difference between using force in developing consequences and using strategies in leading to student empowerment. Again, it is the difference between learning obedience or responsibility.

A major concern often expressed when individualizing consequences is the fear that students will fault professors for being unfair if students are treated differently from one another. However, this is true only for professors who use punishment. These professors are forced to punish consistently as students are usually quick to remind them of classmates who were punished differently for committing exactly the same offense.

Consequences should not be designed to punish students. By definition, *Judicious Consequences* are designed to take into account individual differences among students in order to meet the emotional and learning needs of each person involved. Being educational in nature, students who misbehave simply may have different ways of learning from their mistakes, and, as a result, different consequences are necessary. Two students experiencing difficulty in math would not necessarily both improve their math skills if given the same instruction; they will likely react or learn differently to that instruction or any other single learning strategy. It only makes sense, then, for professors to employ different educational consequences as they work with the many different individual needs and attitudes students bring to behavioral problems.

Although a mentoring approach to behavioral problems is sound professional practice, unknowing students are going to question the inconsistency of professors' actions. It is important to respond to these inquiries in a professional manner, without revealing the confidentiality of the matter. Getting back to the lab work experiment scenario, a professor's response to the student who did clean up the experiment might sound something like, "I have found from the other student's response that there are some other problems we are going to have to discuss. We are going to be working this out and it will be handled in another way." The student who cleaned up the experiment will know the consequences designed to change an attitude will only begin with the other student and that they are both in the hands of a capable professional.

When students perceive their consequences as educational in nature, feel they make sense for them, and are allowed to act on their own volition, they may show little interest in comparing what they are learning from their misbehavior to that which others may need to learn.

Timing is very important to sustain good communication between students and professors. For example, professors should make every attempt to respond to problems as soon as possible, to avoid the discomforting ambiguity that accompanies students' misbehavior. A quick response not only spares students the mental anguish of something being held over their heads, but allows them to experience some immediate control and responsibility for rectifying the situation. There is also something cleansing about getting past unpleasant experiences quickly and putting things back on track again. This is also equally true for professors; both parties are usually relieved when a difficult episode is successfully resolved. As some say: what you resist persists and what you look at disappears.

As with other student behavior problems, students fighting and vigorous arguments can be approached as a manifestation of a personal problem between students who need professional assistance. If counseling, mentoring, and mediation resources are available and consistently carried out, students, professors, and the community will be fully aware that "something positive is being done" about the situation, and at the same time the students involved will not miss valuable classroom activities.

Some professors argue that judicious consequences are not tough enough and therefore will not deter students from misbehaving. Many feel that in the "heat of the battle" hearing students out and working through problems seems to be an undue burden for which there is too little time. In the short run, there may be some validity to these arguments. But when that window of opportunity presents itself, professors can little afford *not* to take the time necessary to help each student progress and grow from their misconduct. In the long run, professors spend much more time judging, reminding, coaxing, confronting, demanding, lecturing, lamenting, conjecturing, and cajoling, than they would taking the time and effort needed to develop attitudes of respect and responsibility.

In summary, professors often wonder why some students seem to enjoy finding out what they can get away with, but others behave in an entirely different manner. We have come to the conclusion that students find no fun at all trying to disrupt learning environments in which they perceive their professors are making every effort to empower them with a shared responsibility, treat them as significant, and allow them to gain confidence in their ability to handle their own affairs.

The Compendium:
Professors and Democratic Classrooms

Democracy is a unique social system with fundamental principles that give all individuals human rights; and those human rights are to be respected by all and protected by the government. So, on the first day of class it should be commonplace to hear professors introduce themselves to their students and to conclude their introductions with a statement like, "... and I am here to protect your human rights." In these few words professors define a student/educator relationship that establishes their role as loyal, helpful educational leaders working with and for each and every student in the class.

Most students have some awareness of what their human rights are, but they typically have not been in a classroom where their rights have been respected and protected. When professors begin the first day of class by recognizing and protecting students' human rights, they have just introduced the first three of ten fundamental principles that are at the heart of *The Judicious Professor* and that provide the structure and framework for developing and maintaining a democratic classroom.

In a democratic classroom students learn their human rights consist of three foundational principles: freedom, justice, and equality.

Freedom—students are able to be themselves and have the right to express themselves through their behavior and opinions. Professors have a responsibility to protect and respect students' individuality and acknowledge their right to make choices.

Justice—students have a right to rules and consequences that are fair to everyone. Professors must ensure that course and classroom expectations are fair; and that any consequences connected with student misbehavior are complementary and commensurate with the contravention of classroom and course guidelines. Students also have the right to adequate notice, to tell their side of the

95

story and to appeal summative decisions to higher authorities. When professors listen to students' concerns and consider their views, they demonstrate a sincere respect for a student's sense of self worth and do much to preserve the ethic of hearing each student's voice in the class.

Equality—students have a right to an equal educational opportunity. Professors need to meet the individual needs of every student in order to give each a chance to succeed in class. Equality does not mean treating every student the same. It means professors will respond to students' individual needs so each will have an opportunity to succeed.

It all begins with the professor, who acts as a representative of government. Professors must be cognizant of respecting and protecting student rights as they develop course syllabi. They will also need to teach about student rights as the course unfolds. In the democratic classroom, the professor will give these rights to all students; human rights are not earned and they are not privileges; they are presented to every individual who "touches the soil" where democratic principles are practiced. Respecting and protecting student rights is most important as students should first identify with their own needs and desires as they are being empowered with the *language of civility*.

The *language of civility* is a balance of rights and responsibilities. Students need to know their human rights can be denied when they exercise individual rights that interfere with the welfare needs of others. In other words, students cannot say and do anything they want; expression and movement are limited by the welfare needs of government. Legally speaking, if professors can demonstrate a *compelling state interest*, the individual rights of students may be denied.

There are four legal arguments used in courts to protect the welfare needs and interests of government. The four legal arguments are:

Threat of Property Loss and Damage: an interest that acts as steward for the care and appropriate use of individual and state owned property.

Legitimate Educational Purpose: an interest that keeps in countenance administrators', professors', and the educational institution's license to make arbitrary decisions that are based on sound educational practice and the mission of the educational institution.

Health and Safety: an interest that serves a fundamental purpose of government to protect the health and safety of students who attend public institutions of higher education.

Serious Disruption of the Educational Process: an interest empowering educational institutions with the professional responsibility to deny student rights that *seriously* disrupt student activities.

As students learn to think and act using these four arguments as guiding principles, the language used in the classroom moves from autocratic talk to democratic talk. For professors, it replaces telling students how to behave with reminding them about their civil responsibilities. For students, it replaces obedience with responsibility.

Students will learn how these four compelling state interests can deny their human rights as professors use them, when developing course syllabi and in course implementation. Student responsibilities will be articulated with examples unique to each course, depending upon content, physical space, the students, and methods employed, but consistently with over-riding guiding principles. The guiding principles are:

Treat All Property with Respect (Threat of Property Loss and Damage): Most students understand the need to protect property and usually have no problems with rules and decisions that deal with personal or public property. Computers, equipment, chairs, desks, and other classroom materials would be examples of community property that must be protected and is entrusted to the care of students. In addition, students will want to discuss and develop guidelines regarding the respectful use of personal property, e.g., borrowing pencils and paper or other resources from other class members.

Take Responsibility for Learning (Legitimate Educational Purpose): This is license for professors to make clear rules and decisions based on their professional judgment. These rules and decisions may appear fairly arbitrary to the uninformed student, however, they are based on professional knowledge and experience and are designed to help students learn. Educational curriculum, teaching methodology, assessment, out-of-class work, assignments, and testing are all examples of decisions professors make based on professional judgment as they carry out their mission and professional responsibilities. These decisions sometimes conflict with the rights of students. For example, teaching about evolution may violate a student's right to freedom of religion if his or her religious beliefs oppose the theory of evolution. In this case, the student would be excused from the classroom when theories of evolution are being taught. On the other hand, curriculum policies based on legitimate educational purpose can mandate that every liberal studies student successfully complete English 101, denying students' academic freedom of choice. Such rules and decisions must be both legitimate and educational to legally deny students' rights.

Act in a Safe and Healthy Way (Health and Safety): One of the principle roles of government is to maintain a healthy and safe environment and students must take this responsibility seriously. Clear and published guidelines about every individual's physical health and safety on campus are essential to ensuring a safe and secure learning environment. This principle includes not only physical health and safety, but emotional and psychological health as well. Students who tease or harass may be affecting another student's emotional health. Vulgar language or bigoted slurs heard in class or printed on clothing are not constitutionally protected speech. Reminding students of their responsibility for the emotional health of others is an empowering approach to creating a consciousness of tolerance and respect among the student body. Health and safety must become the concern of both students and professors, not by forcing the issue, but by using the power of knowledge, language, modeling, discourse, and awareness to bring about a community of mutual respect.

Respect the Rights and Needs of Others (Serious Disruption of the Educational Process): Problematic in teaching and learning about this principle is the definition of "serious." Classroom disruptions can vary greatly from one classroom to the other depending on such differences as class size, subject matter, age, teaching methods, classroom conditions, and the professor's teaching style. Expressing and discussing the various factors which can affect a good learning environment generally result in ownership by everyone and does much to avoid disruptive classroom behaviors. Students usually agree material disruptions can interfere with their education; however, they are also often ready to dispute the seriousness of such disruptions. Facilitating class discussions can be an effective approach for determining mutually agreed upon standards of responsible behavior.

Three more fundamental principles used in the court cases are *reasonable time*, *place*, and *manner*. "Time, place and manner" are used as criteria in deciding whether government has abused its authority in denying or moderating individual rights. For example, if a student is contacted on a cell phone and he chooses to answer it during class, the professor can ask the student, "Is this is the best time, place, or manner?" When the fundamental principles of time, place, and manner are taught to students, they make great organizers for balancing individual rights with the rights and interests of others, and the professor simply uses this organizer to remind students of their responsibilities, thus avoiding confrontation. By asking questions about reasonable time, place, and manner, professors reinforce responsible thinking in students who are beginning to use these fundamental principles as organizers for an intrinsic rationale, and it helps them to think about what it means to be a responsible citizen in a free, democratic society.

The following ten principles:

Human Rights:
(1) Freedom,
(2) Equality, and
(3) Justice.

Student Responsibilities:
(4) Threat of Property Loss
    and Damage,
(5) Legitimate Educational
    Purpose,
(6) Health and Safety,
(7) Serious Disruption of the
Educational Process.

Reasonable;
(8) Time,
(9) Place, and
(10) Manner.

are fundamental to democratic practices and processes, and they are the essence of the *language of civility* that is used in the democratic classroom. For example, when students engage in heated discussion, instead of admonishing students for verbally harassing one another with a statement like "Stop bullying each other," professors and students can remind the verbally abusive students of their responsibilities by asking "Is there a better way you can say things so as to respect the health and safety of others?" Or if a student is misusing class furniture or equipment the professor can replace statements like "That's no way to act," with asking "Is there a property issue here?" Questions that include reminders of student responsibilities avoid confrontations with students by separating professors from the rules and thus relieve professors of playing an authoritarian role and telling students how to act. Refreshing a students' memory emphasizes the power contained in a guiding principle and avoids the use of personal power which often results in counterforce from the student. When professors use the language of civility to empower students with an intrinsic sense of responsibility, they find their students begin to move away from an obedience mindset to one of autonomy and self-control.

Respecting students' rights and asking them to exercise them responsibly by setting up the rules or behavioral guidelines for the classroom, allows students to become stakeholders in the operation of the class and take responsibility for its proper functioning. A community of learners emerges that will balance, maintain, and further develop the classroom culture within the fundamental principles of a democratic classroom. As a result, professors may not feel personally violated when students misbehave and go beyond the bounds of behavioral expectations set up by the class members. Professors can separate themselves from rules because they are based on democratic principles and the language of civility and not their bias' and idiosyncrasies.

As a consequence of separating the rules from the professor, professors will seldom find themselves in a power struggle with students. When students mess up or stray from the class guidelines, the professor simply maintains that same professional posture consistent with helping students deal with problem situations. If professors are going to be effective in helping students recover from their misbehavior, get back on track, and do something else the next time the problem occurs, they need to maintain a student/professor relationship that engages students in problem-solving. We refer to this mind-set as a *"professional relationship"* approach to rules and consequences.

A *"professional relationship"* is defined as a fiduciary relationship in which students are entrusted to the care of their professors. The professional ethics of this relationship is for professors to always act in the best interests of those in their care, and the proof of this ethic is that every student believes that professors are always acting in his or her best interests. This is not easy for professors to bring about in an educational setting unless students are included and feel a sense of responsibility in maintaining the class culture. *Professors must include students when developing the class rules and guidelines.* This "front loading" does much to help students take responsibility for classroom culture and the maintenance of good working relationships with other students and the professor. The professional relationship relies heavily on student ownership of class rules and guidelines and the achievement of mutual academic goals. So, when students find themselves in noncompliance with *their* class rules and expectations the relationship with the professor can remain intact if the professor does two things to support and maintain a professional relationship with troubled students.

First, avoid language and strategies that can lead to adversarial relationships. Steer clear of lecturing students. Language like, "I told you not to do that again" and "You should be ashamed of yourself" are usually voiced to make professors look and feel responsible. Pointing out mistakes students already know about and retelling them what they have heard many times are examples of professors forcing the issue with guilt trips and threats in hopes of bringing about compliant, submissive, or passive students. If students are going to learn to be responsible they should be doing the talking and not be responding defensively to moralizing lectures. So, stop lecturing!

Second, avoid judging students. Playing judge and jury is a "criminal justice" approach that often humiliates, punishes, and pushes students away from the learning community. Professors must learn to accept students exactly where they are now, assuming they have done their best. This does not imply that professors need to agree with what misbehaving students have done, it simply establishes a "professional relationship" with the student much like that of a doctor/patient or lawyer/client relationship. Students are not asking professors to approve of what they have done; they are asking for a professional educator to trust and understand that their behavior was genuine and, under the circumstances, what they thought they needed to do at the time.

In the "professional relationship," the first words spoken to a troubled student are always in the form of a question. The person doing the talking is the one who is responsible. The question allows students to respond with their side of the story and invites them to tell about the situation, recall what happened, explain, make predictions, and put forward possible choices based on recollections and predictions. This question and answer discourse encourages the use of intellect and critical thinking and when conducted in a non-judgmental fashion it leads to mutual respect and the acknowledgement of responsible behavior for both students in trouble and professors.

Professors who use a "democratic approach" to setting up rules and classroom guidelines separate themselves from the rules and make it possible for straightforward talk about rules without becoming defensive. By the same token, it is also more likely students will talk about their problems if professors separate students from their misbehavior. This can be accomplished with the language we use to discuss the problem situation. By avoiding "why" questions and focusing on questions related to "*What happened?*" professors do much to separate the student from the misbehavior. "Why did you…," for example, focuses on the "you," which often leads to defensiveness and litanies of excuses from students. Whereas, "What happened?" asks students to describe "what" occurred. "Would you like to talk about it?" also emphasizes "it" and thereby helps students avoid feeling they will be judged by the professor.

Once students have had an opportunity to respond (and regardless of what they say), the next question to be discussed is, "*What needs to be done now?*" This discussion revolves around what students need to do to put things back together and make them whole again. It is the legal concept called "*restitution.*" Restitution involves the restoration of property and relationships. So, it is important that misbehaving students consider the feelings of others and if feelings have been hurt, a discussion regarding an apology would be a "first step" toward restoring

103

relationships. As well, property needs to be restored and professors may help students by asking questions about how they can repair the damage, e.g., "What do you think needs to be done to fix the chair?"

When students have come to some resolution about what happened and what needs to be done, the professor asks, *"What can we learn from this?"* Questions and discussions should relate to changing goals and attitudes and talking about what can be done next time so this will not happen again.

It is important that throughout the whole discussion of consequences, professors always respond to students in the form of questions. If students are reluctant to respond to questions or have no ideas, professors could ask questions introducing their own ideas for student consideration. For example, "What do you think about doing ____ now?" or "What would happen if you did ____ next time?" or "Do you think an apology would help the situation?" Decisions emanating from these "leading questions" must be volitional on the part of students, all the professor is doing is providing some ideas that the student may not have considered. The important feature of this conversation is that students must feel they are making their own decisions and not playing off the authority of the professor. Troubled students are truly fortunate to be in the professional care of a professor committed to helping them recover and get back on track with their education.

Guidelines and decisions based on democratic principles and consequences grounded in a professional relationship help bring students to a principled level of thinking. As a result, it is more likely that students will become more self-directed and able to take responsibility for learning. They will display flexibility in a variety of social situations without demanding conformity of all students and they will be able to empathize with others and establish mutual expectations based on respect for themselves and others. A democratic classroom is about developing learning goals with students that are designed to enhance character and courage and that provide them a presence of mind for living a life of equability and self-control.

Chapter Six

A Synthesis and Evaluation of Legal, Ethical, and Educational Issues

This chapter is the synthesis and evaluation of student constitutional rights, good educational practice, and professional ethics counterbalanced with the problems and practical realities of classroom leadership. Although some of the subject matter examined may appear to have little to do with good leadership, the subtle nature of discriminatory practices cuts deep into students' feelings of self-worth and is often the cause for putting students at risk of dropping the course or quitting higher education altogether. For instance, how many times would a professor have to repeat or just listen without confronting jokes demeaning a student's ethnicity or sexual orientation before students lose confidence in that professor, or become sullen or despondent, or begin patterns of disruptive behavior? Too often it is an unthinking and insensitive professor who spawns and serves as the lifeblood of an uncaring and hostile classroom environment.

The dynamics of balancing rights and responsibilities require professors to stay abreast of new laws and good management practices in an effort to meet society's increasing demands on public colleges and universities. Professors must not only consider and fairly represent the demands of the majority, but also remain conscious of and respect the rights and feelings of individual students. This chapter provides professors with a sensible, consistent, and judicious rationale for rules and decisions affecting student learning and behavior.

Grading Practices

The letter grade on a transcript is generally perceived as the student's level of skill and understanding of the subject matter. Because past academic achievement and the skills they represent are critical to predicting success, students' grades are used often by educators and employers as a basis for deciding future opportunities.However, due to the excessive entanglement between *achievement* and *behavior*, achievement grades are often misinterpreted.

For example, an academically gifted student whose grade is lowered because of absences, late papers, or a bad attitude in class could likely be deprived of future employment or schooling opportunities. As a result, professors' grading practices may violate a student's Fourteenth Amendment right to liberty by following a practice that passes along misinformation which puts in jeopardy future opportunities.

Notwithstanding the authority professors have to determine curriculum and standards for grades, a student's future opportunities must not hinge on what the professor thinks the grade means, but what the widespread consensus of those who interpret the grade think it means. For example, lowering a grade for a late assignment in a creative writing course would be different from lowering a grade for missing a deadline in a journalism class. Whereas learning punctuality in order to meet press time could be an expected achievement in the field of journalism for a grade in a journalism class, it would not be considered as a measure of achievement for those interpreting a grade in a class on creative writing.

Therefore, it is important to incorporate in the academic grade only those requirements and standards commonly understood by "the profession" or the community at large to be course content. A plausible test would be to ask employers, other professors, and experts in the field what they believe an "A" or a "C" means in a specific course of study. The liberty issue lies not in what the grade means to the professor or the student, but that it *communicates to the reader* an accurate statement of the student's academic achievement.

Although behavioral information is very important to those deciding on the future opportunities of students, it should be passed on separately through other means. The most effective form of disclosing behavioral information is through discourse, where questions and clarification between interested parties allow them the best chance to flesh out relevant and pertinent information. A distant second best would be written statements describing facts and events about student behavior directly related to the matter in question. Letter grades and check-lists simply allow for no give-and-take, which opens even more possibilities for miscommunication.

Professors often cite "real world" reasons to lower grades, for such things as tardiness, poor attitude, or late assignments. They argue that these and other similar behavior patterns can often lead to being fired from jobs and that having students experience this lesson in school will prove beneficial to them later on when they are in the workplace. How many times have professors said in this context, "You will thank me some day for this"? However, many of these students who are continually late to class are never late for their job. Lowering achievement grades for misbehavior does not always teach responsibility, but it does always pass on misinformation.

Students are still *learning* promptness and a cooperative attitude. They should not be experiencing an employer/employee relationship with their professor; indeed, in the workplace such relationships are often adversarial. Instead, students should be experiencing a professional relationship with their professors, who are using educational strategies designed to develop and change attitudes and goals. Furthermore, students in public colleges and universities have liberty rights, but employees in the private sector do not.

Employers have discovered it is not good business to fire someone they have spent time and money to hire and train, only to have to go through the process again with someone else. They have also learned that employees' productivity and attendance are not related as much to fear of dismissal as to the positive aspects of personal accomplishment and pride in the product or service. The law today requires management in business and manufacturing to help workers who are experiencing problems in the workplace by offering them assistance, such as counseling, rehabilitation, retraining, and educational help. Until employers have, in good faith, tried to help a troubled employee succeed on the job, they cannot legally dismiss them. If this educational approach is good for business, then the concepts of judicious grading practices are very much in line with the "real world" of business and industry.

Late Assignments

The approach professors use to handle late assignments reveals immediately whether or not they are learner-centered. By accepting and not grading down late work, professors send a professional message to students that completing assignments, receiving the professor's feedback and being fairly evaluated are all important to their educational success.

Conversely, professors who do not accept or who grade down late assignments generally have two reasons. They argue: (1) administrative convenience—that unless penalized, most students will hand in all their work at the end of the grading period, not leaving the professor adequate time for grading; and (2) teaching responsibility—that students should learn to be responsible for getting work done on time because this is what is going to happen to them in the "real world."

These contradicting philosophies were a source of frustration to a former graduate student who returned to visit with one of the authors several years after completing her degree. As an experienced English teacher, she had always reasoned that with many papers to grade, a strategy was needed to pressure students to complete their work on time; she feared the alternative would be a deluge of papers at the end of each grading period. Even though she continued her policy, she always had the feeling that there was something not fair about lowering grades on well-written papers. When she re-examined the issue in light of student liberty interests, she knew she had to find another approach. After trying several alternatives that did not work, she finally settled on the following plan.

She begins her class with a review of the course requirements, one of which is a short composition due every two weeks. She continues with an explanation that these assignments will be evaluated and returned within a few days. She expands on the educational value of writing practice, learning from mistakes, and the benefits of her feedback. In addition, she informs the class that she has over one hundred fifty students a week and has budgeted just enough time to correct and return papers handed in on schedule. She emphasizes that it is to their educational advantage and her administrative convenience for compositions to be submitted on a regular basis.

Next, she points to two boxes on her desk; one labeled "papers on time" and the other "late papers." She informs her students that papers coming in on time will be corrected and returned as promised; late compositions will be processed and returned as time allows, or possibly sometime next term. If she cannot get to them, students can expect an "Incomplete" in the course until she can read the papers.

In other words, late papers...late grades. She smiled when she told how she now has very few problems with late papers. No longer does she constantly have to remind students of deadlines or grade down good writing, and, as a result, more of her students are doing their work and accepting the responsibility for turning in their work on time. As a footnote, some educators using this two-box system have added a third box for "early papers." They report that some students really like the early box and that it also provides an opportunity to get a head start on the papers.

Late assignments are something professors can quickly turn into positive learning experiences for students as well as for themselves. Inquiry may result in professors finding that students do not have the skills to do the assignment, or their personal life is such that it just could not get done. Some students have little experience meeting deadlines and really need help learning how to organize their time and to set goals for themselves. By turning late assignments into learning experiences, professors move immediately from the role of enforcer to that of educator. Professors who accept late work tell us that students are more likely to complete their assignments if they know it will not be graded down, thereby learning and benefiting more from the coursework. It also communicates to students that all class assignments have a legitimate educational purpose that must be fulfilled. Many educators are also discussing due dates for assignments with students based on how much time they feel the student will need to complete the work. Taking into account the students' needs and interests gives them some ownership in the deadline. As one author attests, a student scrawled this testimony on a course evaluation, "I liked knowing that I could hand in my assignments late, with no penalty, but I got them all in on time, out of respect."

But there are those who argue that accepting late assignments is unfair to other students, because more time has been allowed to complete the assignment. However, if all students are allowed the same chance to hand in late assignments, then all will have the same equal opportunity to give the assignment their best effort. We think that a statement placed in the syllabus, like the one below, allows all students the opportunity to do their best work on class assignments.

The assignments, presentations and analyses are all designed to help the student certify her or his understanding of the knowledge and concepts covered in class and the required reading. Completed assignments will be assessed and graded by the instructor. Details of the assignments are documented in the syllabus and will be further explained by the instructor during class or on an individual basis by appointment. The assignments are due on the specified dates published in the syllabus. All assignments will receive written comments and an academic achievement grade from the instructor and will be returned to the student as soon as possible, if the student turns the course work in on time. If it is late, *no grade penalty will apply*, but the instructor will provide written comments and an academic achievement grade when time is available for the instructor to deal with late course assignments. Be sure to hand in your best work.

Some professors fear students will take advantage of this approach and hand in all assignments late. Many professors believe only problems will result from placing so much responsibility in the hands of their students. Almost all who try this method of accepting late work, however, discover their fears to be unfounded. Instead, most experience a sense of professional pride in the fact that their students are now completing their assignments without all the prodding and loss of interest associated with late work penalties.

There is something antithetical about an educational assignment that, when late, is not accepted by a "professional educator." The assignment was made in the best interests of the student's educational success, and if not accepted, the student's interests are simply not being served. Students suddenly get the feeling their professor does not really care about their success in class and has simply given up on them. The message being sent to students is that being punctual is far more important than the educational value of the coursework assigned.

While an early/on-time/late box solution may not work for every professor, it is one example of how to handle late assignments in a way consistent with goals of fostering academic ability and achievement. In addition, it creates an environment in which students experience personal accountability while at the same time it models the professional responsibility of professors.

The Incomplete Grade

Administrators who encourage and allow professors the judicious use of the "Incomplete" grade offer their professors an opportunity to be fair and accurate in their grading practices. This option does not have the effect of diminishing class rigor, and sends a message to students that until all assignments and tests are complete, they will not receive a grade or credit for the class.

Prudent administrative policy would allow a reasonable time for students to make up required work. This "reasonable time" could vary depending on the student's need for course credit or the availability of the professor involved.

If course work is not completed within a reasonable time frame, the incomplete grade or "IN" should remain an "IN" or be changed to a "NG" (no grade) or a "W" (withdraw). However, changing an "IN" to an "F" would imply the student did complete the course work, but failed to understand the subject matter or meet the course standards, thus sending an incorrect message. An "IN," "NG," or "W," on the other hand, would not misinform the person interpreting the transcript and would simply mean the student did not complete the course. The "IN," however, could have a beneficial effect on marginal students. The difference between telling students that they did not finish the course or that they failed could be the difference between deciding to continue in school or not.

In the event an "IN" needs to be changed to an achievement grade, such as for graduation purposes, a grade could be compiled from the information available. If in the professional judgment of the professor there is enough evidence to determine the student's mastery of the subject, the grade could be negotiated with the student at that time. Whether the student receives a grade and credit should always remain the professional judgment of the student's professor, based upon reasonable course expectations.

Other Behavioral Issues in Grading Achievement

It is sometimes very difficult to separate *student attitudes* from achievement grades. Most professors will agree that it is easier to grade fairly students with good attitudes who are always on task and in class than it is to remain objective when assessing less attentive or rebellious students. When professors' insecurities concerning their expertise or authority get bruised, the tendency is to want to retaliate against students by grading them more harshly.

However, objectivity and fairness in grading are very important to student liberty interests. Although it is sometimes very difficult, professors must somehow get beyond the fact they have been hurt by a student's poor attitude. This really takes practice with some students. But by not thinking about previous behavior and focusing intently on helping all students succeed academically, it can become a well-earned intrinsic reward.

It is common practice for students caught *cheating* on exams or *plagiarizing* assignments to receive an "F" for their work. This is often averaged with their other grades or used as the final grade in the course. The problem with this practice is that an "F" connotes academic achievement (or lack of it) and will be interpreted as such by those who read it. Because cheating and plagiarism are behavioral issues, rather than academic indices, they should be treated separately.

This is an excellent opportunity to work with students on the problems that lead up to the act of cheating or plagiarizing itself. For example, a student caught cheating on an exam could be offered a make-up exam, possibly the same one given to students who did not take the test due to illness. By the same token, plagiarizing should entail completing another paper or report covering the same topic. Professors must separate fair and accurate evaluation from their professional responsibilities aimed at getting to the real issues of student misbehavior.

In addition to providing for alternative academic evaluations and requirements, students should be on notice from the first class meeting that cheating and plagiarizing are serious behavioral matters. It is important for students to know from the beginning that exemplary as well as deceitful conduct will have an effect on how others will evaluate them. In some instances their future opportunities in school and career opportunities may be at stake. Although achievement grades will not be affected, there will be conferences about the problem and consequences designed to resolve the issue. Professors will not only be much more effective in holding together the teaching and learning relationship, but will be protecting student liberties in the difficult arena of cheating and plagiarizing.

Whether to use *norm-referenced* or *criterion-referenced grading* reflects the educational philosophy of every professor. In norm-referenced grading, the other students in the class provide the norms for determining the meaning of a given individual's grade. This is sometimes referred to as "grading on the curve," where there is only a limited number of each grade awarded. Teachers using this type of competitive grading do not provide an equal educational opportunity for all students to be graded on what they have achieved in the course.

Criterion-referenced grading, on the other hand, is when achievement is not compared to that of others, but rather to a given criterion or standard of performance. This is a learner-centered grading philosophy and allows everyone an equal opportunity to pass specific course standards. In theory, all students could receive a high grade if they in fact achieved the relevant course criterion. Although all students seldom receive the highest grade, this grading practice is by definition encouraging to students and gives them the message that their professor is truly working in *each* student's best interests.

Class attendance is often commingled with the academic grade. Every professor knows when students miss class they lose the benefits of learning that occur in the normal course of classroom activities. But instead of grading down for non-attendance, educational alternatives should be developed and required that are closely related to the classroom discussions and activities missed during students' absences. It is common for professors to prepare learning assignments for students going on a pre-arranged extra-curricular activity or for students absent due to an extended illness. The same approach could be used as educational alternatives for those who have been absent.

Other examples of educational alternatives for absent students might be doing the coursework collaboratively with a tutor/teaching assistant, writing a short paper covering the subject matter discussed, a book or chapter review on the subject, or several pages outlining the missed chapters discussed in class. To alleviate the overload generated by educational alternatives and make-up work, academic departments should provide tutors/teaching assistants and schedule times when help would be available. Well-planned alternative assignments not only offer students their right to an equal education, but emphasize the importance of class rigor and academic expectations.

In the event that alternative assignments are viewed by some students as punishment for being absent, a clear explanation would be necessary to illustrate that it is an educational expectation in lieu of what other students learned in class. The difference could be that students considering whether or not to miss class might think, "Do I want to learn the course material in class, *or*, do I want to learn the course material doing an alternative assignment?"

Professors who ask, "Are you telling me that if a student has been ill and another was skipping, that they should both be able to make up the work that they missed?" Our response is that both students needed a professor when they returned, perhaps the one who skipped class more than the other. Regardless of the reason for the students' absences, make up work and late assignments should be accepted to ensure those students an equal educational opportunity.

Excused and unexcused absences are not relevant to an achievement grade. There is no legitimate educational purpose for distinguishing between excused and unexcused absences. For educational purposes, therefore, there only needs to be recorded absences. Those absent, for whatever reason, would simply make up the missed class experience with alternative learning assignments or other mutually agreed upon learning activities.

This approach avoids the difficulty professors are faced with when trying to decide whether a student is actually ill or that there was in fact an emergency situation that kept them from attending class. Checking the validity of excuses is at best unmanageable and often leads to an adversarial confrontation over the veracity of the student's word.

Students are unfortunately conditioned over the years to plead and sometimes lie as they explain absences or request exceptions. We are always amazed by the relief on their faces when we interrupt students in the middle of their unsolicited excuse by saying, "I respect the decision you have made not to be in class. You may tell me if you wish, but we also need to talk about other ways for you to cover what the rest of us went over in class." Invariably their attitude becomes one of cooperation and interest in what they had missed.

Class participation is often used as a criterion because professors fear students will not willingly interact in activities and discussions and therefore must be coerced. It typically gives an advantage to certain learning styles and personalities who are good at speaking up. Students who are shy, reflective in their learning style, suffer from a speech disorder, or have previously been embarrassed by wrong answers are only a few examples of those who may be reluctant to participate openly in class discussions.

There are better ways to help students participate. Inviting students to interact through inductive teaching techniques, brainstorming, a Socratic teaching style, listening carefully to and recognizing the value of what each student has to say, and breaking the class into small discussion groups are just a few strategies that will encourage student participation. Professors who want to avoid being discriminatory as well as embarrassing students should simply eliminate participation from their achievement grade. Some exceptions would be classes such as speech, music, and foreign languages.

Figuring student *effort* into an achievement grade is highly subjective and not related at all to skills or knowledge of the subject. Effort is a behavioral matter and usually denotes motivation and interest in the course content or class activities. If information about student interest, motivation, and effort is important to pass along to those concerned with class achievement, this should be done by using oral or written statements specifically describing behaviors. Using achievement grades to motivate students may appear at first to be professionally responsible; however, when the inflated grade passes along misinformation, it affects the integrity of the communication to the reader.

Improvement is also not relevant to achievement. Improvement implies a change, but it does not provide baseline data or explain to what extent the student improved. However, communicating effort and improvement to interested others is very good feedback. It is often the motivating force behind students setting and reaching higher academic goals. Although this feedback is crucial to students' success, it must be communicated by other means than through the achievement grade.

In addition, effort and improvement grades sometimes have the appearance of being inequitable to students. As an example, a student related an experience she had with her grade in one of her science classes. She had earned 79 points and received a "C", just missing a "B" in the class by a single point. Her roommate also earned 79 points but received a "B".

When she talked to her professor about this inconsistency, he explained to her that her roommate improved more on the second test than she did. The reward for this improvement was the higher grade. The student laments to this day, "How can anyone with so much education not understand that two students who have the same 79 understanding of the subject, must be given the same achievement grade?" The ambiguity and disconnectedness of figuring in improvement is not fair nor is it relevant to student achievement.

Extra-credit coursework would be fair only if it were offered equally to all members of the class at the beginning of the course. Near the end of the grading period, students occasionally will ask for extra-credit assignments or to re-take tests in order to bring up their grades. Unless this opportunity is announced and made available to the whole class, allowing a few students to make up for lost ground would be denying other students an equal opportunity.

When extra-credit assignments are allowed, they should add to student knowledge and skills within the proper context of the course content. They should not involve activities that are not academically relevant, such as grading papers, cleanup activities, or doing errands.

Grading down for *misspelling or poor grammar* in non-language classes poses an interesting contradiction. On one side of the argument is the question of whether all professors should have the educational responsibility for teaching and requiring good writing skills. The answer, of course, is yes. Writing ability and spelling are important to every student's education and should be monitored by all professors. The contradiction arises from whether students' poor communication skills should be averaged into the final grade in non-language classes.

Let's use the example of a student who hands in a science paper that is outstanding in every way except for numerous spelling and grammatical errors. Grading down for the language errors would misrepresent the student's understanding of science. But to allow the student to hand in an assignment replete with writing errors would be professionally irresponsible.

The answer is to get away from the thinking that professors need to grade everything they require. Instead of grading down, for example, poorly written papers might be returned for appropriate corrections and accepted only when good writing standards are met.

Although these other approaches would meet the immediate need of correcting writing errors, perhaps it should also be made clear that along with mastery of course content, good communication skills will be an expected part of the class rigor and integrated throughout the curriculum. It is very important that students get the message from all their professors that the ability to communicate well is valued throughout their personal and professional life.

Grades should accurately reflect the *final measure of achievement* in the course. Unsatisfactory coursework at the beginning of the class averaged with demonstrated ability at the end could misrepresent the student's final skill level achieved. For example, in courses such as writing composition or art, figuring in poor grades for early, less successful work would distort the final measure of achievement at the end of the grading period. Professional judgment allows for a more holistic approach to assessment.

And finally, *grading homework, papers written outside class, portfolios*, and *take-home exams* beg the question of whose work is being graded. This is one of the most frustrating issues professors face. On the one hand, class time is very limited, and therefore outside time must be used in ways that will enhance student understanding of material. Conversely, as educationally sound as outside assignments are, the work turned in does not necessarily represent valid evidence of individual student achievement.

Homework assignments are inherently unequal. The inequalities within the classroom are numerous enough, but outside the classroom there exists very little equality in educational opportunities. But in spite of this inherent inequality, many professors do grade homework. Although homework is often not completed for any number of reasons, most of these professors are convinced that grading is the threat needed to get the work done.

The problem is that grading homework not only fosters cheating, but it has the effect of pushing students out of higher education. How many students are "sick" or skip class if they do not have their homework completed? How many students copy the work of others or have help from others? How many students are doing their homework the hour before it is due? And who wants to go to class only to be embarrassed by professors making examples of students not completing their homework assignments?

To bring about more equity, as well as more learning, professors must learn alternatives to grading homework. The best way to begin is to view homework in terms of learning goals and avoid using homework for performance goals. With *learning goals* (task-involved), the issue for students is to improve and learn, regardless of mistakes or how foolish they appear. They seek challenges and persevere. With *performance goals* (ego-involved), students are concerned about how they are judged by others. They often experience anxiety, are likely to avoid difficult challenges, and give up when they fail. To illustrate, the following are some ideas for learning goals and ways to motivate students to complete outside assignments:

1. *Bring up the assignment's due date for class discussion* as a way of having students feel responsible for meeting the deadline. When the whole class agrees on a reasonable time for the work to be completed, a lot of weight is shifted from the professor's shoulders to those of the students.

2. *"Busy work" is obvious to students.* Professors could place the responsibility for learning on students by allowing them some authority in the assignment. For

example, assign thirty problems and ask students to practice as many as they think they need to understand the concept. This communicates a message to students about the importance of practice to bring about understanding as well as trusting in their ability to assess their own learning.

3. *Encourage cooperative efforts among students* when doing homework as a way of stimulating interest in the assignment, and suggest peer coaching for students experiencing problems. Tutors and teaching assistants, and classmates can provide easily available and often helpful resources.

4. *Take time to get students started* on homework assignments before they leave class. Sending students away from class with an assignment they do not understand or do not have the ability to do is very discouraging. When it is started in class, professors can diagnose potential problems and students get home knowing how to do it, and are often motivated because they have part of their homework already finished.

5. *When homework is due, it should be discussed that same day*, with each student checking their own work. Not giving proper class time to homework indicates it was not important. Also, exchanging homework with another student violates student confidentiality as well as denying them the best opportunity to get immediate feedback on what they have done.

6. *Use homework for diagnostic purposes.* It is an excellent way to learn if the teaching methods being used are effective in addition to identifying students experiencing trouble with the material.

7. *Approach homework not as something students have to do*, but as something they *get to do* to enhance their understanding and experience the joy of learning new knowledge.

Tests and quizzes are normally about performance, while *cooperative testing* is a strategy that pursues learning goals. Beginning the session before a weekly quiz, give each student a small index card to use as a "cheat sheet." Each student can write as many notes for the quiz that will fit on the card. Then, assign partners in class to take the quiz together next session. Explain to them that when taking the quiz, students can work together to answer the questions and they can only use their "cheat sheets," nothing else. Have students change partners each week, allowing them to work with as many different students in the class as possible. We think you will find that everyone's grades will improve on mid-term and finals which students should take individually. The success on these tests stems from the amount of effort students put into the "cheat sheets" each week. Motivated by wanting to "help" their partner, students are doing much to help themselves. This strategy also works to reduce test anxiety as students learn how to take tests by sharing their study strategies and test-taking strategies with other students in the class. Their cooperative grade on the quizzes can be a small part of the final grade, but a big part of the learning that goes on in the class. Professors should find that few students will miss "quiz day" because they have a responsibility to a partner and missing the quiz would leave their partner to take the test alone.

Determining whether *term papers* are actually each student's own effort can sometimes be very difficult. Writing style and knowing a student's previous work is helpful, but not always a valid test. The more an assignment requires personal experiences and their own thinking, the less likely students are to solicit outside help. Reflecting understanding is always fundamental to any paper, but requiring personal opinions and conclusions that demonstrate the ability to synthesize and evaluate make plagiarizing much more difficult. The difficulties in determining students' work are also true of *portfolios*. Help from professors, tutors, and helpful friends many times add something to the mix which can misrepresent a student's real abilities.

Take-home exams are used most effectively in smaller classes where professors have other means of establishing levels of achievement. Much can be learned about students in classes where there is plenty of interaction and individual ability has an opportunity to surface. The take-home exam then becomes more of a culminating activity that summarizes the important aspects of the course and confirms the suspected achievement of individual students.

There are some advantages to take-home tests. They can be more comprehensive than in-class tests, give students as much time as is needed to complete them, and are an educationally sound method of learning subject matter. Because it is common for students in the class to cooperate and help each other, take-home exams are great learning experiences, but they do not always accurately represent the individual understanding of students.

Make sure that course requirements are stated clearly in the syllabus. For example, the course requirements for an educational law course might look something like this:

Course Requirements: Course requirements are based on learning goals which involve the following tasks:

Read the assignments set out in the course calendar.

Brief for the class cases assigned to you.

Attend class regularly.

Write a 6-8 page paper synthesizing and evaluating legal and educational issues you believe are currently relevant to you at this point in your professional development. Emphasis should be placed on meaningfulness to you as you develop legal awareness and use this awareness to re-contextualize your professional goals and practices.

Final examination is the concluding task in the learning process. The exam is for the purpose of feedback to you and to me as to what we were able to accomplish in the context of the learning and teaching culture we established in this class.

Evaluation and Assessment: Grades will be determined by the professional judgment of the instructor using feedback from students' satisfactory completion of the demonstrated achievement of the tasks set out in the course requirements.

It is also helpful for the professor to view the student as an active participant in the assessment process. Invite and value self-assessments and act on them as bases for assessment, evaluation, and reporting. A standard statement in your syllabi can invite dialogue and value a student's self-assessment. For example, here a professor has assigned students to write a self-assessment for the course:

> *Self-Assessment for this course:* Your written self-assessment should be expository in nature. It should indicate an anticipated letter grade for this course. Provide reasons why this letter grade is appropriate to communicate to a wider audience the summation of your academic achievement in this section of the block. The self-assessment should document and certify through examples what you know and how you are able to apply that knowledge.
>
> Your self-assessment should be written about you. It can address affective, cognitive, and physical effects and affects. It can address the course requirements. It can include comments you have received from others. It can include goals you set for yourself and the extent to which these goals were achieved and how those goals correlated with the expected outcomes of the course.
>
> There is no "right way" to write your self-assessment, but remember the self-assessment is about your academic achievement. Writing a *self-assessment* is sometimes confused with *course evaluation*. While self-assessment is an important part of the course evaluation, other vehicles are provided for you to evaluate the effectiveness of the course. So, please ensure that the self-assessment is about you.
>
> Ultimately it is the responsibility of the instructor to award the grade that you have earned. Observable behavior is only one indicator of what has been academi-

cally achieved. That is why you are asked to share this responsibility with me and to indicate behavior, cognition, and feelings that I could not have observed or may have misinterpreted.

When appropriate, professors may allow students the opportunity to redeem their work. But, this can soon become unworkable as students continue to hand in their work until they receive a desired grade. On the other hand, professors can encourage students to share their assigned work with each other during the first part of class when the assignment is due; this allows them an opportunity to do a quick self-assessment as they share their ideas with others in the class. Then students can decide whether they need to redo the assignment or if it is truly their best work and it is ready for the scrutiny of the professor. Such a practice speaks loudly to the student that there is no grade penalty for late work, and that this work is important, and that quality work is important, so don't hand in your completed work until it is your best work, ready for assessment.

In conclusion, professors should make every effort to ensure that grades are an accurate reflection of student academic achievements. The balance between the need for professors to use an achievement grade to control behavior and the students' need for accurate assessment must tip in favor of students' liberty interests and their right to the future opportunities they have earned.

Property Loss and Damage

Reasonable rules protecting community property are usually well accepted by students. If a problem occurs, it is often because students have not received *adequate notice* that their actions were damaging to the college's or university's property or the property of others. For example, students who are not properly instructed about the nature of computers or scientific equipment used in their classes may find nothing wrong with fiddling around with it just to see if they can get it to work. Students also may be unaware of the fact that furniture and equipment should be left in the room assigned and not carried off to other rooms for others to use. Identifying and discussing foreseeable problem areas at the beginning of each class will undoubtedly lessen the likelihood of misunderstandings and embarrassment resulting from lack of information. Adequate notice and proper instruction are essential to a fair and reasonable policies designed to protect property.

Judicious consequences for *damage to college or university property* should be consistent with and proportionate to the severity of the loss incurred and the students' genuine feelings of remorse. Professors should communicate with offending students about the logic as well as the legality of making *restitution* for property damaged or stolen. Equipment or materials not returned could also result in *loss of privileges* associated with the activity. For example, a volleyball not returned would result in the loss of athletic equipment privileges until it is returned or replaced. Although many institutions of higher education have a "security deposit" which is used to pay for breakage and missing community property, this should be used only as a last resort. If the damage to the classroom or equipment is coming from the students in the class, professors could hold a discussion on the topic to talk about the problem and ways it can be alleviated. If the source of the problem seems to be coming from outside the building, class discussion could focus on the possibility of improving classroom security, everyone keeping an eye out for trespassers, and other kinds of community activities designed to alleviate the problem.

The loss or damage of any *student's personal property* is always a matter of concern for institutions of higher education. Students should be informed that bringing personal items to the college or university could result in their loss or damage. Students should understand that every effort will be made to help them care for their belongings, but that the institution does not have adequate supervisory staff or security personnel to ensure the safety of all their personal effects. Especially if there have been problems in the past, professors should make every effort to inform students at the beginning of class about the problems of personal property being stolen or even borrowed by others and even discuss possible ways to prevent this from happening.

Rules relating to community and personal property should be

perceived by students as a proactive approach to responsible behavior, with judicious consequences designed for the purpose of changing attitudes and goals. This requires professors to teach and promote an attitude of pride in the facilities and respect for the property of others. Class discussions, posters around the building, and occasional complementary and encouraging remarks are a few more ways to help students build and maintain good feelings about their educational community. Graffiti boards established throughout the campus just for the purpose of extemporaneous expression would be a visual message to students that graffiti is inevitable, but let's do it in a way which does not damage property.

A positive educational approach designed to create a protective and caring attitude among students for community and personal property will, in the long run, be far more effective than living in fear of rigid rules and punishing consequences. Then, all who enter a classroom for the first time know immediately how the people who teach and learn at the college or university feel about themselves and others around them. Democratic principles employed by vigilant and resourceful professors can be quite successful in bringing about a classroom relatively free from intentional acts of property loss and damage.

Speech and Expression

Speech and expression issues on higher education campuses can take many forms, one of which is student *dress and appearance*. Colleges and universities are best served by one broadly written rule communicating the importance of dress and appearance appropriate to the learning and living environment on campus. The message should be one of respect for the students' ability to decide reasonable appearance in a higher education setting. Students whom school officials believe are going beyond reasonable bounds could be handled on an individual basis. In each case, students should not be barred from wearing what they choose unless it is *discriminatory* or *pervasively vulgar*, and until all advising and conference avenues have been exhausted. Exceptions to this general rule would be in programs where the students are participating in practicum classes and internships and are learning and modeling the appearance standard set out by the profession.

Occasionally, students or professors feel uncomfortable and complain about offensive *speech or appearance of other students*. In cases where the language or appearance of other students is not discriminatory or pervasively vulgar, professors could take that opportunity to help those disturbed by the display to understand that an individual's language and appearance are considered forms of self-expression that are protected by the 1st Amendment. Professors should take the time to help their students understand individual expression from a constitutional perspective. Beginning with a forum for students to communicate and learn from each other, where appreciation of how other individuals view the world on a campus with differing opinions and rich cultural diversity. is a great way to start the dialog.

Insubordination and open defiance of professors not only violates college or university policy, but is personally infuriating and often difficult to handle without taking it personally. Those in the helping professions should learn ways to control emotions and not personalize insolent attitudes, but interpret such behavior as symptoms of other more serious problems. For example, a student who stands up in class and says, "You don't know what you are talking about. This whole class stinks and so do your lectures," may simply be reacting to a poor grade on an exam or problems that have been developing with a roommate.

A visceral reaction of an angry statement in kind by the professor would only make things worse. In this case, professors must try to avoid a confrontation by using a more judicious response, such as, "Do we need to talk about this now or can it wait until right after class is over?" By responding this way, the professor would not be backing down or condoning the student's statement, but exemplifying a professional demeanor and the empathy needed to help a student who may be experiencing a very bad day. The immediate problem is obviously a defiant attitude, but to modify student's attitudes and keep them in higher education means getting to the source of the real problem. This can only be accomplished at another time away from the group setting and within the context of a confidential "professional relationship." However, if the whole group becomes defiant, then it must be handled immediately by involving everyone in the group in a discussion. If it gets out of hand, admit it right away and talk about resolving the problem at another time at the next class session.

Not every form of student speech is protected by the 1st Amendment, *only ideas are protected*. For example, profane language, indecent gestures, and bigoted statements directed at someone and intended to harass have no protection within the meaning of the Constitution. Racial epithets, gender denigration, religious vilification, and cultural disparagement are only some examples of expression which would lead to a serious disruption of the educational process as well as affect the emotional health of the students being harassed. A classroom discussion setting out examples of sensitive issues would be a good way to help students learn that freedom of speech does not give one license to harass others, and at the same time gives them an opportunity to learn that ideas and opinions are encouraged.

For example, a sign stating "Saddam is gay" appeared at one university on a residence hall window during the Gulf War crisis. The hall director took this opportunity to have a hall meeting which included members of the Gay and Lesbian Association on campus expressing their views about how the statement made them feel. Student attitudes were expressed openly on all sides, which resulted in a growing and learning experience for everyone in the hall. Those offended by the statement learned that opinions and ideas were protected by the 1st Amendment and many students in the hall that evening learned to be more sensitive about homophobic issues. Because it takes time to process and reflect on new information and simply get beyond the point of defending what was once believed, not all students will become more tolerant after just one meeting. Therefore, time for change must be allowed and continued effort must be made toward helping students understand the value and ways of tolerance. When the sign came down it was because attitudes were changed and not because of a mandate from the hall director.

As repugnant and distasteful as these incidents are, they must be met head-on with judicious resolve and leadership in order to bring about a learning experience designed to enable everyone to grow and change. Again we turn to the words of the *Tinker* decision for guidance.

> ... *in our system, undifferentiated fear or apprehension of disturbance is not enough to overcome the right to freedom of expression. Any departure from absolute regimentation may cause trouble. Any word spoken, in class, in the lunchroom or on the campus, that deviates from the views of another person, may start an argument or cause a disturbance. But our Constitution says we must take this risk; and our history says that it is this sort of freedom—this kind of openness—that is the basis of our hazardous national strength and of the independence and vigor of Americans who grow up and live in the relatively permissive, often disputatious society.*

Student demonstrations seem to surface periodically and when they do they usually enjoy a high profile due to the publicity they receive. Because of this notoriety and students right to demonstrate, professors should openly embrace and support this form of student expression and do everything necessary to help carry out a non-disruptive and safe demonstration. This is a good opportunity to talk with students planning a demonstration about their 1st Amendment rights balanced against their responsibility of a reasonable *time, place and manner* for such an event. For example, students planning a sit-in near the dining hall entrance area to protest the quality of food served need to learn the *manner* of leaving room for others to enter the dining hall. Those who plan to chant loudly outside the Administration Building about the quality of classroom instruction on campus need to be aware of the best *time* or *place* so as not to disturb classes or students studying.

Often what students have to say or how they express what they have to say is *offensive to others*; at least, it could be what most would consider to be "in bad taste." Years ago when some institutions of higher education were considering pulling their investments out of companies doing business in South Africa because of their apartheid policies, some students at a small college built a small shanty village next to the administration building. The village was made mostly of cardboard and scrapes of old pieces of wood holding it precariously together. It looked ramshackle and unsightly as planned, reminiscent of some villages in South Africa. Here in the middle of a beautiful, wooded campus was this "eyesore" speaking more loudly than all the flyers and posters proclaiming the same message. It stayed there for months and near the end the weather and neglect caused it to look even worse. As professors would come to campus each week to teach, they were constantly reminded how an "eyesore" allowed to remain there transforms into a thing of beauty as it works so profoundly to bring the campus community to a more principled level of thinking. It soon became more than just an expression by students about South African politics; it became a statement by the administration about the importance of free speech in a civil culture.

Professors could encourage independent thinking and a vigorous exchange of students' ideas by providing bulletin board space in the classroom for various *free speech activities*. We do not need less expression on campuses, we need more students and professors speaking out on issues important to them. For example, consider the effect of a single flyer stapled to a bulletin board expressing a bigoted statement directed at a minority group of students. The one statement would have quite an impact on those readers passing by and could possibly have them thinking to themselves, "This is certainly a bigoted campus." On the other hand, picture that same bulletin board with the same bigoted statement now cluttered and overflowing with other flyers, signs, and posters expressing all sorts of different viewpoints and opinions on all kinds of topics. The effect is quite different. Although the bigoted statement remains, most see it now in a more realistic context and are more likely to be thinking, "There must be a bigot living on campus."

It is very important for students to feel they have a public forum to speak out on issues of personal interest and public concern. By providing free speech bulletin boards, the institution of higher edcuation is balancing student rights with the school's need to control the reasonable time, place, and manner of student expression. In the words of the *Tinker* decision:

> ....*this sort of hazardous freedom...this kind of openness...that is the basis of our national strength...must be balanced with states' interests in providing an educational environment free from serious disruptions.*

Professors and administration should not act precipitously or without serious deliberation on issues of student speech and expression. With such an important freedom at stake, professors should take the time to help students learn the responsibility that goes with expressing themselves. And just as important, develop in other students who are provoked and disturbed by certain ideas, the patience and understanding for those who are exercising their constitutional right to speak out.

Search and Seizure

Occasionally, professors have reason to search students who they suspect are concealing such things as books, community materials and equipment, drugs, or the personal property of another student. In most instances the professor just wants to recover the property and return what was taken to the rightful owner. In order to accomplish this, professors often take it upon themselves to summarily open backpacks or clear out storage lockers in an effort to locate missing items. This somewhat heavy-handed approach has now given way to students' rights under the Fourth Amendment, which require professors to search for and seize suspected contraband and prohibited items only if they have reasonable cause at the inception of the search and if it is within a reasonable scope of the incident that prompted the search.

The *Fourth Amendment* of the United States Constitution forbids "unreasonable searches and seizures" by government officials and provides that warrants "describing the place to be searched, and the persons or things to be seized" can be issued only "upon probable cause." This amendment is applicable to public institutions of higher education when a state or federal criminal prosecution is based on evidence obtained from college or university premises and professors or administration are involved. An illegal search by a professor will likely bring into play the Exclusionary Rule used by courts to exclude evidence illegally seized. The rule, simply stated, means that evidence acquired in a manner that violates a defendant's constitutional rights is not admissible in a criminal trial.

Evidence acquired in a manner that violates the 4th Amendment centers on what is "unreasonable." The reasonableness of the search must be measured carefully against the probable cause requirement and society's legitimate interest in preserving the privacy, integrity, and dignity of its citizens. Although some courts have applied this rule to college disciplinary procedures, the trend is away from excluding fruits of an illegal search at suspension and expulsion hearings.

The *"plain view" exception* to the 4th Amendment is an important aspect of reasonable searches. The 4th Amendment only protects one from a search and seizure of property which is concealed, therefore allowing anything in plain view to be seized and legally admitted into evidence. Crucial to this exception is that the professor, at the time of the viewing, is legally present or acting in accordance with the law. For example, if a professor of health science, while walking through the locker room, sees in plain view evidence of stolen athletic equipment through the open door of a student's locker, it would not violate the student's constitutional rights for the professor to enter the locker and seize the stolen property. By being in the locker room legally and observing the illegal substance through an open locker door, the plain view exception made the seizure legal.

The *four compelling state interests* can be used as the legal rationale to gain entry to students' lockers, backpacks, or residence hall rooms. For example, college or university rules should stipulate that entrance to space maintained by the institution, such as lockers, classrooms, and living quarters, will be carried out on a periodic basis for reasons of health and safety (inspect for cleanliness) or property loss or damage (periodic inspections for damage to room or misplaced property). These "housekeeping" type of entries are fairly common and students must be given adequate notice as to when they will occur. These regulations, based on the college's compelling state interests, must be narrowly written to permit legal entry and the search must be conducted for only the reasons specified in the rules.

In general, administrative *entries must be made in good faith* and directly related to the welfare of the college or university. They simply cannot be an administrative ploy to circumvent students' 4th Amendment rights, with the underlying purpose being to look for possible criminal activity. It is very important to advise students there will be periodic searches and notify them in advance when and for what reasons the searches will occur. This open and straight forward approach not only adds to the integrity of good administrative practice in the eyes of the students, but reduces student suspicions that professors and administration are "sneaking around behind their backs."

Whenever possible *have students present* when conducting the search. If students are not present, professors risk possible accusations of taking something else from a room, backpack, or locker, or just invading a student's privacy. When students cannot be present, ask another faculty member to witness the search and the possible seizure of the student's property. Professors should leave a message stating their purpose for the search and a receipt for any property that was seized. Although students may give up some of their rights to privacy, they do not give up their *right to notice*. If something is found to be missing in the building, a *random search* of all students' lockers, backpacks, or rooms is not advisable and could be a constitutional infringement on their rights. On the other hand, if there was probable cause to believe that a specific student was concealing the missing property, searching that one student's locker, backpack, or room would be legal.

A common practice is to *take student property* that is being disruptive or not allowed by the campus rules. Stereos, dangerous weapons, and animals are but a few examples of things occasionally taken and held for the student. Although these items may be properly disallowed, professors and administrators who confiscate property and do not return it within a reasonable period of time are similarly blameworthy by committing a "tortious taking of another's chattel." Students' personal property should be returned as soon as possible, with the exception of illegal items and dangerous weapons. Illegal drugs, firearms, or contraband taken from students should be turned over to campus security or law enforcement authorities immediately. When doing this, ask these officials for a receipt listing the items submitted. Having a receipt could protect you from the embarrassment of accusations that you kept the student's property for yourself.

It is also a good idea for faculty to *give receipts to students* when property is taken from them. Providing a student with a receipt connotes legality to the action and has the appearance of valuing student's property, as well as providing a record of what and when it was taken. Consider the hypocrisy of summarily taking something from a student as modeling exactly what students are asked not to do—that of taking property from other people. By issuing a receipt, what could appear to some as a strong-armed act becomes one of showing respect for the personal property of students. The issue here is one of judicious leadership style and not a question of who has the authority.

Students who *refuse a reasonable request* to relinquish something they are concealing must be handled with caution. Wrestling students to the floor in order to search pockets or back packs may not only result in injury, but be construed later as unreasonable force. Professors confronted with this situation should not attempt to physically search or seize property, but should rely on the assistance from other security staff or deal with the problem at a later time. If students continue to resist and there is danger involved, call immediately for campus security or law enforcement personnel.

In *emergency situations* where the health and safety of those in the building is endangered, the law allows greater latitude for institutions of higher education to conduct a legal search. In matters of campus security, law enforcement or emergency personnel should be brought in immediately. In these situations, searches may be legally conducted on the spot, notwithstanding the fact students are not present or a search warrant was not obtained. For example, in the case of a bomb threat a search of students' lockers, backpacks lying around unattended, or smoke coming from a student's room would be examples of such emergencies. Law enforcement officers are in the act of performing their legal responsibilities in searching for a bomb and when they find drugs in a student's backpack, they may invoke the "plain view doctrine" as they seize the illegal substance. During times of crises affecting the security of the community, as the examples illustrate, the civil rights of students often have the appearance of being abated until the danger has passed.

Although professors do not have a license to search randomly or invade the privacy of students, they do enjoy the administrative authority to conduct reasonable searches and seizures. By following the campus guidelines, professors have all the legal support necessary to manage successfully a safe and secure learning environment. Professors who understand and apply 4th Amendment concepts judiciously should experience few student complaints and feel a greater sense of confidence when dealing with a student's expectancy of privacy.

Press

The 1st Amendment freedom of the press clause was set forth to prohibit *prior restraint*. Simply stated, our government does not have the legal authority to mandate in advance what anyone may or may not publish or distribute. However, if a publication injures another person, remedy is through a civil action for libel. In addition, publishing material which advocates the violent overthrow of our government or which is obscene may result in a criminal prosecution. Civil and criminal actions both may supervene the publication, and wrongdoing will be decided on the merits of each situation. Therefore, the basic freedom of the press question which faces college and university officials is whether prior restraint or censorship can legally be applied to student publications. As a general rule, the answer is *it cannot*.

In a campus newspaper published by the student press, for example, the college authorities could not publish rules or make decisions on what the students can or cannot publish. Unless students in their classroom have their own publication, professors are involved for the most part with questions of their students as well as outsiders who want to *distribute materials* in the classroom. These may be in the form of books, pamphlets, or leaflets representing many different kinds of ideas and opinions. As with other freedoms, the distribution of these materials may be regulated by the professor to a reasonable *time, place, and manner*, but they cannot go so far as to require the prior approval of the message, ideas, or subject matter of the publication. In other words, there can be no prior restraint, such as not allowing the expression of ideas on abortion, flag burning, or other issues which the professor feels might provoke students.

Time, place, and manner regulations can be formulated by using the *four compelling state interests as guidelines*. For example, nailing or tacking leaflets into walls would damage community property, distributing materials during a lecture time would be in violation of legitimate educational purpose or a serious disruption, passing out obscene or pervasively vulgar material could affect the emotional health of some students, and bigoted or "fighting words" could be harassment and lead to a serious disruption. By using society's rationale for deciding reasonable time, place, and manner, the personal feelings and biases of professors are not likely to be in question and as a result, professors enforcing these rules have the appearance of being personally removed from value judgment decisions. This is especially helpful to remaining self-assured and poised when talking to students who are frustrated and upset when they are restrained from disseminating publications they believe they had a constitutional right to distribute. Although students may not always agree with the decision, most will comply with well-informed and fair professors doing their best to balance society's welfare with the human interests and rights of their students.

There are two very difficult areas faculty must deal with in the distribution of published materials—obscenity and libel. It is clearly within the authority of professors to ban obscene and libelous publications. In order to deny the distribution of publications, procedural safeguards must be carefully crafted and constructed to focus as narrowly as possible on the content to be censored.

Obscenity on campus is not easily defined and should not be envisaged as "in the eye of the beholder" or as "I know it when I see it." The personal taste and bias of professors should not be the determining factor; the standard for the campus community is the same as that of the general community. The language for these guidelines comes from court cases deciding on the merits of many different fact situations. These guidelines tend to be quite broad in nature, but give us some language we can use when examining the content and explaining our decision to inquiring students. The following is one example:

... *A state offense must be limited to works which, taken as a whole, appeal to the prurient interest in sex, which portray sexual conduct in a patently offensive way, and which, taken as a whole, do not have serious literary, artistic, political, or scientific value.* . . . (Miller v. California, 413 U.S. 15, 24 (1973)

Prurient interest is a phrase used often in court decisions defining obscenity and is generally interpreted as "having or expressing lustful ideas or desires."

Students do not have a right to publish or distribute *libelous materials*. In order for the statement to be libelous, it must be more than just false or misleading. One must prove intent to maltreatment. It also must cause at least nominal injury to the person libeled and be attributable to some fault on the part of the person or organization publishing it. Predicting whether distributed material will be libelous is very difficult since injury and intent is only speculative and often difficult to prove in court. Moreover, public figures have higher expectations of false and misleading statements and thereby would come under a higher fault standard. Professors, for example, would be considered public figures and therefore would come under this higher fault standard. Demeaning statements or outlandish caricatures of professors published by students to lampoon authority figures simply must be "taken with a grain of salt" and just considered as part of the job. Because of its complexity and emotional cost, professors should approach suspected matters of libel with caution. If there is a question about the statement, move it up through administrative channels and possibly to the institution's legal advisor.

If students are denied the right to distribute published material, they should be informed about their *procedural due process rights*. To restate briefly, the procedural due process rights of students are notice, a fair hearing, and an appeal. Applied to student press matters, *adequate notice* means material not permitted (obscene and libelous) for distribution must be stated in a manner that is clear, concise, and reasonably understood by the students. *A fair hearing* means that the reasons for students not being allowed to distribute the publication must be heard and considered before the decision is conclusive. Finally, the student has the *right to appeal* the decision at the hearing, as well as other decisions rendered in the appellate process.

Because college faculty must make decisions based on what they believe is obscene or libelous, telling students immediately of their due process rights will usually work to avoid an unnecessary confrontation. A statement such as "I'm sorry you feel that way, but I am going to have to remove your poster because I feel it is libelous to some members of this campus community. If you would like to appeal my decision, you should talk to the Department Chair." This avoids an adversarial interaction and has instead the appearance of helping disappointed and sometimes angry students work within the system.

One of the objectives of the college experience should be to teach the importance of a strong press in a democratic society and, through example, how an educational administration, professors, and student body can accept and learn from a free and open exchange of ideas. An open and above-board discourse of student and professor's opinions should be encouraged and viewed by the administration as an indicator of a healthy educational environment. If authorities disagree with students' viewpoints, they can easily disassociate the college or university from the substantive views expressed by stating or publishing a disclaimer. Students who object to the ideas being distributed by their counterparts should be encouraged to express their views in a similar manner.

Professors must maintain a delicate balance between students' rights to publish and distribute their opinions with the institution of higher education's need for responsible student behavior. Unreasonable or heavy-handed attempts at censorship of student publications quickly escalate and is often a feature news item in the local press, and on occasion, receives national attention. The fourth estate hangs together very well, vigorously guarding its freedom from prior restraint and thirsting to champion even the smallest of publication injustices. Higher education authorities must make every effort to avoid any unnecessary and unthinking confrontations with student press, or for that matter, any press. Judicious decisions matured by responsible substantive and procedural due process procedures help everyone learn to appreciate this fundamental right so important to our nation's heritage.

Religion

The First Amendment to the Constitution provides that "Congress shall make no law respecting an *establishment* of religion, or prohibiting the *free exercise* thereof." When applied to student rights, this double-edged sword forbids public institutions of higher education from establishing religion, and, at the same time requires the colleges and universities to accommodate the free exercise of its students' religious practices and beliefs. Because professors are sometimes heavily involved with religious questions of their own as well as those of their students, knowledge of church-state legal issues could be helpful.

A clear, workable legal perspective on religious discrimination begins with an understanding of the application of the tripartite test developed by the Supreme Court over many years and brought together in Lemon v. Kurtzman, 403 U.S. 602 (1971). *First*, the statute must have a *secular legislative purpose*. Secular purpose usually translates into legitimate educational purpose when applied to most higher education issues. *Second*, its principal or primary effect must be one that *neither advances nor inhibits religion*. In other words, professors must remain neutral and cannot celebrate or advocate a religious point of view, nor can they take a hostile attitude toward religion or impair its worth. *Third*, the statute must not foster an *excessive government entanglement* with religion. There must be a real and ostensible separation between religion and the state. Entanglement matters usually involve control over the use of federal funding and decision-making authority. Campus rules, decisions, and activities must pass all three tests if they are to meet the constitutional criterion of nondiscriminatory practices.

Although the tripartite test is fundamental to decisions on religious issues, the constitutional concept to keep in mind is the difference between the establishment clause which prevents professors from establishing religion, and the free exercise clause which allows students to freely exercise their religious beliefs. For example, individual students who choose to have a Christmas tree as well as other Christmas symbols on their lockers or in their rooms would be *freely exercising* their religious belief. But on the other hand, professors with the same decorations in their offices and classrooms could be making a statement that *advances* their religious belief, thereby violating the establishment clause. The difference between the two is that offices and classrooms of professors serve a public purpose designed to carry out the states' educational responsibilities, whereas students' lockers and rooms are legally theirs for their own personal use and, in the case of religion, to freely express their religious beliefs.

This, of course, begs the question of professors and their rights within the meaning of the free exercise clause. Professors do have some free exercise rights, but they must be carefully balanced at all times with their professional responsibilities as a government employee, who by law is not permitted to advance or advocate a religious point of view. It is common to most colleges and universities that there are many religions and cultural traditions represented in their student bodies. Professors, therefore, who flaunt their cultural and religious beliefs, put in jeopardy the appearance of respecting and accepting others who do not share those same beliefs. This appearance may seem subtle, but it is essential to the integrity of a viable teaching and learning relationship.

Professors must be discreet about expressing their personal feelings regarding religion. A small nativity scene or Menorah placed unobtrusively on a professor's desk might have the appearance of only a personal expression of religious belief; one, so to speak, that is being interpreted by others as saying, "This religion is good for *me*." On the other hand, a professor's office filled with religious symbols and decorations could be very intimidating and have a coercive effect on students coming into the office for advising or academic help. The message here to others would be, "This religion is good for *everyone*." It is very important, therefore, for professors to conscientiously balance personal religious convictions with professional responsibilities.

Students are quick to recognize the difference between a professor's personal right of expression, religious as well as other personal ideologies, and a professor who has the intention of imposing their belief on others. Judicious professors will be respected and approachable as advisors and mentors to students of all faiths as well as to nonbelievers. The balance lies in being very prudent about personal religious beliefs, with that of being cognizant and respectful of the religious convictions of others.

College or university religious decorations or prayers have the appearance of the institution advancing religion through celebration or worship and for that reason would seem to violate the establishment clause. However, invocations and benedictions in Congress or at city council meetings as well as Christmas decorations on public property have been held by some courts not to violate the 1st Amendment. These prayers and religious symbols in the public sector have been held constitutional only because they passed the test of being designed and implemented for a secular legislative purpose, thereby meeting the standard set out in the *Lemon* case. Ceremony, tradition, and its "solemnizing" function are the most common reasons cited for "secularizing prayer" at public functions as well as "simply a tolerable acknowledgement of beliefs widely held among the people of this country."

These legal arguments are often used as the basis to allow invocations and benedictions at college and university functions as well the "traditional" Christmas tree as a *secular statement* reminding students of a religious tradition upon which the coming student holiday is based. As long as it has a secular purpose, it should withstand the establishment test. In other words, students who ask to decorate the classroom or student lounge, should use symbols depicting the advent of winter vacation as their dominant theme, such as snowflakes, skis, sleds, snow people, families getting together, and a big sign reading "Happy Holiday." A Christmas tree, Menorah, and other religious symbols displayed as part of the decoration would appear as only a reminder of religious traditions celebrated during this time of year and should not have the effect of being there for the purpose of advancing those religions. Just as an aside, a "limited open forum" has now been established and the same area used for these decorations should be made available for other student expressions throughout the school year.

Part of the pain in all aspects of discrimination is the lonely feeling of being "left out." It can appear very lonely to the one who feels outside, and can be all the difference in the world between enjoying and benefiting from campus life or being turned off and completely discouraged by the system. Not unlike other discriminatory practices, religion too can be the source of frustration and despondency if not handled properly by professors and administration.

Discriminatory Practices

The Fourteenth Amendment, from which all discrimination laws emanate states in part: "...nor deny to any person within its jurisdiction the *equal protection of the laws*." From this brief clause federal and state law makers have enacted enabling legislation which protects students from discrimination based on race, national origin, religion, sex, age, disability, and marital status. In addition, federal and state agencies have promulgated numerous administrative rules which govern discriminatory practices. This section is not a review of these many laws but a reminder of how a professor's bias and prejudice can have a detrimental effect on students' human rights. Professors unaware and insensitive to ethnic, cultural, and status issues and who are unappreciative of the unique differences among students are more likely to speak and act in ways which result in unequal treatment of students. Only when professors begin to model and teach the qualities of character which make a diverse nation possible, have they met their professional responsibilities as well as the demands of equity in a culturally diverse society.

Professors, who seldom stereotype or label others, appear to understand and value the background, culture, and unique differences among their students. These professors embody qualities which enable them to:

Expect the same standards of personal conduct and academic achievement from all students regardless of their gender, ethnic group or cultural tradition.

Avoid comparing or ranking groups with respect to behavior, attitudes, and accomplishments.

Avoid the use of descriptive terms, stereotyped phrases, or participation in humor that is derogatory or demeaning to any group of people.

Promptly admit errors in judgment, sincerely apologize, and are willing to learn new perspectives.

Integrate classroom displays, assignments, and lectures with various people in different roles.

Maintain eye contact, smile, stand near, and enjoy being a professor to all students.

One problem facing colleges and universities today is the *sexual harassment* of students by professors as well as between students themselves. It is important for professors to understand that it *is the difference in authority*, not the intentions of those involved, that transforms offensive behavior into sexual harassment. The assumption is that because of their position and the power professors have over students to decide their future opportunities, students will have a tendency to feel they must acquiesce to invitations and agree to requests for favors. Therefore, no matter the intentions, professors just asking a student for a date or even to have lunch with them, unless it is directly related to classroom concerns, are behaving in a manner which comes within the meaning of sexual harassment.

Sexual harassment, as in other areas of the law, does not lead itself to specific limits. It is contextual in nature and much depends on the people and the circumstances in each situation. Although there is no legal definition of sexual harassment in education, we must look to federal regulations governing the workplace for guidelines.

Unwelcome sexual advances, requests for sexual favors or other verbal or physical conduct of a sexual nature constitute sexual harassment when (1) submission of such conduct is made either implicitly or explicitly a term or condition of an individual's employment, (2) submission to or rejection of such conduct by an individual is used as the basis for employment decisions affecting such individual, or (3) such conduct has the purpose or effect of creating an intimidating, hostile, or offensive working environment [EEOC Interpretive Guidelines on Discrimination Because of Sex Under Title VII, 29 C.F.R. 1604.11 (1984)].

Examples of sexual harassment include acts such as sexual assault, displays of derogatory images of women or men, direct propositions, subtle pressure for sexual activity, unnecessary touching, patting, or pinching, verbal harassment or abuse, leering at or ogling of a student's body, and sexual innuendos or jokes about a person's sexual orientation. The effects of sexual harassment or harassment of any nature on students can be overwhelming and have a devastating effect on their success in higher education. With the current campus atmosphere concerning female student safety, and the heightened awareness of the area of "acquaintance rape," sexual harassment is a major concern on college and university campuses today. Professors

144

who are dismissing their night classes, for example, could inquire about safety concerns students might have in leaving the building or getting home safely.

In and around the office or classroom there may be *joking and harassing behavior* which not only affects those who are the target of this humor and harassment, but often can create a hostile and anxious teaching and learning environment. Whatever form harassment takes or the reason the person is being victimized, it can lead to illness, loss of confidence, decreased concentration, diminished ambition, and depression. In cases of bigoted taunting and teasing, professors must act immediately and take an active part in bringing about a judicious resolution. If discriminatory acts and statements are not quickly handled, they are likely to get out of hand and result in wounds to people which will never heal completely.

In addition to harassing language and actions, professors must be conscious of the appearance of their classrooms and offices. Just as with excessive religious symbols and posters that make some students feel uncomfortable and dissuade them from entering, the same is true of expressing other subject matter which might be offensive or in poor taste. For example, students would have a right to a lewd poster in their room, but the same poster in a professor's office would be a discriminatory practice, as well as neglect of their duty as a professor. Professors' classrooms and offices must be a model of tolerance and sensitivity to discriminatory practices, not only as an example for others to follow, but to provide a comfortable and respectful place to carry on teaching and learning activities. If professors are viewed by all as being resolute in their stand on discrimination and not as a part of the problem—respect, appreciation, and equanimity will soon follow.

Professors who fully comprehend and believe in the concepts of freedom, justice, and equality are going to encounter fewer problems. Students who feel accepted and understood by those in authority usually have second thoughts about not attending class or taking part in needless disruptions of the learning environment. Professors spend too much time talking and interacting with students to think they can pretend they hold attitudes which they do not. Few study professors more, or know their biases and weaknesses better, than their students. Students are keenly aware that the words professors use are only symbols representing what they want others to believe. When words say one thing while gestures and actions another, this is often the antecedent of putting at risk the trust and concern needed for a strong teaching and learning relationship. *The Judicious Professor* requires a genuine commitment and conscientious effort to assure all students an equal opportunity to enjoy and benefit from their college or university experience.

Health and Safety

One of the important functions of government is the protection of its citizens. This duty is even more important when colleges and universities, through their professors and administration, are vested with the duty of protecting students from unreasonable risk arising out of the professional student/educator relationship. The importance of student health and safety occasionally surfaces in a lawsuit against the institution holding those in authority responsible for their negligent acts. While some students may occasionally complain about not being able to skateboard in certain parts of campus or about having to undergo a physical before entering higher education, most recognize the purpose of these rules and, with appropriate reminders, acquiesce.

In order to be workable and effective, however, rules governing students' health and safety should be:

1. *Well-planned.* (1) Consider what a reasonably prudent educator would have foreseen under the same or similar circumstances, (2) periodically inspect for hidden dangers, (3) develop a plan to prevent those foreseeable problems, and (4) follow through with the plan.

2. *Highly Visible.* Use posters, warning signs, verbal reminders, adequate supervision, and other similar measures to insure adequate notice and control over foreseeable problems

3. *Fully Understood*. Use instructional handouts, verbal explanations, demonstrated student ability, and other communication efforts to teach students the proper health and safety rules, skills, and procedures appropriate for the subject being taught.

4. *Consistently Enforced*. Use proper supervision, be consistent, and "don't even let the Department Chair in the science lab without eye protection."

Professors should take some time to discuss with students the *importance of following rules* promulgated for the purpose of protecting their health and safety and that, without their cooperation, these rules will be very difficult to enforce. As a general rule, there should be a direct relationship between the likelihood of injury and the time and effort devoted to instruction on health and safety precautions. For example, a weightlifting apparatus in a campus center workout room and the technique necessary to use it may require only a posted list of some simple instructions to adequately inform students of its safe use. On the other hand, a geology class on a field trip to rugged mountain terrain would require considerable time and expertise to adequately prepare the participants for a safe outing free from accidents and injuries. Because of the likelihood of student injury on the geology field trip, much more time and effort should be allocated to proper instructions and adequate supervision designed to prevent possible injuries.

Field trips and other *off campus activities* obviously create a greater need for proper instruction and concern for adequate supervision. Planning for activities off campus should take into account the hazards at the site, risks involved in transporting students, the age and maturity of participating students, as well as anticipating other foreseeable problems related specifically to the location and activities planned.

Liability waivers students sign declaring their knowledge of the risks involved may be in order for some field trips and activities. When planning off-campus activities, especially when traveling some distance or the activity could be dangerous, professors should inquire with departmental administration as to the availability and appropriateness of liability waivers. Using liability waivers is an excellent way of making clear to those who are participating any foreseeable dangers as well as providing some protection to the institution in case of an injury.

Students who drive their own cars to classroom or institution sponsored activities, especially those carrying other students, should be instructed to follow reasonable safety rules and confirm the fact they are driving safe vehicles. Faculty should take the time to check student drivers for (1) a valid driver's license, (2) adequate insurance coverage, and, if possible, (3) evidence of a good driving record. Whenever possible, instead of assigning students to student-driven vehicles, professors should allow other students to choose drivers with whom they ride, not only for their own emotional health, but also for the fact that it distances the institutions' responsibility to some extent. For students driving college or university vehicles, simply learn about and follow exactly the institutional guidelines.

Professors have a legal duty to help students under their care who become *sick or injured*. Those who are competent to administer first aid should do so only up to their level of expertise, and then proceed to obtain other medical assistance. Professors not knowledgeable in first aid should immediately act in accordance with a previously-discussed and established plan designed to bring about prompt medical attention. The importance of *following procedures* established by the higher educational institution's administration cannot be overemphasized. If there is a lawsuit filed as a result of an injury, the professor's actions will be judged later as to what a reasonably prudent educator of the same subject would have done under the same or similar circumstances.

Professors cannot afford to compromise on issues relating to students' health and safety. In addition to the tragedy of a student becoming sick or injured, looming in the background is always the threat of a time-consuming and thorny lawsuit as the result of negligent health and safety precautions. If there is a serious injury, professors involved should begin documenting immediately the circumstances that led up to the injury, what occurred at the scene, and any later information coming to their attention. This information could prove very helpful when an accurate account of the facts could become critcally important to the attorney representing the institution. Anticipate and plan ways to handle foreseeable dangers, carry through with proper supervision and instructions, and be consistent with enforcement. If the rule or decision is well thought out and supported by sound professional advice, professors must hold firm and not waver in matters pertaining to student health and safety.

Confidentiality

If there is a vital organ in the body of our Constitution, it is the individual's expectation of privacy from governmental action. There is federal legislation, such as the Family Educational Rights and Privacy Act, as well as separate state legislation that often provide specific guidelines concerning the confidentiality of student records and conversations between students and professors. Professors and college or university staff directly impacted by the rules and regulations governing confidentiality must be knowledgeable of and stay current with the applicable federal and state laws. Where these laws do not apply, the principle of professional ethics should be emphasized and prevail.

Although ethics do not represent the letter of the law, a sense of professional responsibility and conscience on the part of professors must reflect the spirit of student's Constitutional right of privacy. The following recommendations, therefore, have their basis in this fundamental principle:

> Consider all conversations with students and colleagues to be confidential from others, except those who have a demonstrated professional need to know or if the information involves a serious question of health and safety, i.e., suicide, abuse, weapons, etc.

> Take steps to ensure students' academic achievement or behavioral information is not viewed or known by others; i.e., posting of grades, reprimands for rules infractions, etc.

Avoid comments and visible reactions relating to student behavior in the presence of others. Choose an appropriate time, place, and manner away from others for private conversations to prevent from being overheard. Doing this for both corrective as well as commendation purposes demonstrates a concern for student self-consciousness problems and avoids many unforeseen problems related to public disclosures.

Refrain from comparing students with anyone, especially in the presence of other students.

Discourage students who gossip about the private life of others.

Before touching students in any way, give thought to possible ramifications, i.e., reactions of students abused as children, sexual overtures, right to privacy, tort liability, etc.

Student discipline and academic problems are sometimes directly related to a professor *disclosing information* that, in retrospect, should have been communicated privately or not at all. For example, telling a student in front of the class, "Someone whose work-habits are as poor as yours should never be allowed to continue in the program," is hardly the time, place, or manner to diagnose or confront someone about how their personal habits are affecting their continuation in their field of study. Often statements made by professors take the form of a flippant remark or sarcastic comment uttered spontaneously in an effort to be clever or entertaining. Many times a single wanton statement or gesture coming from other students and reinforced by professors, even tacit support, can be just as devastating to the targeted student's feeling of self-worth. Any disparaging statement about a student made publicly, whether or not in jest, has the somber affect of diminishing spirit and the feeling of being valued and, in the long run, often pushes the student out of a class or even out of the academic field of study.

Suicide and other life-threatening disclosures are examples of confidential communications which must be reported to qualified and appropriate college or university authorities. Many student problems are simply beyond the expertise of professors who, while carrying out the responsibilities of their teaching position, become privy to life-threatening information which must be passed on to other professional staff. In these cases, one-on-one advising should be avoided and the student should be immediately directed to someone whose duty and training enables them to work with the problem presented. Although a student in some cases may conditionally converse with a professor, asking him or her to promise not to tell anyone else, in life and death matters or situations that are dangerous to others, the confidential relationship must be abandoned in favor of a professional team approach. This not only will provide better help for the student, but also avoids the possibility of a professor being a party to a lawsuit for malpractice.

Professors sometimes hear confessions by students of past *criminal activity*, such as possessing or selling drugs, assault, stealing, extortion, and other similar illegal acts. In the case of only knowing about alleged criminal activity, the professor is not legally held to disclose the information voluntarily to law enforcement officials. However, professors could be legally implicated as an accessory to the student's subsequent actions if they act and in some way participate in the criminal activity after hearing about the crime. In addition, most states have the authority to subpoena professors to testify in court about the confidential disclosure of the student's criminal activity. Professors must be up front with their advisees and explain to them right away about legal constraints over which they have no control when students begin disclosing this kind of information.

Advising students about abortion, use of contraceptives, conflicts they have with family values, and other similar lifestyle decisions should be done with caution, if at all. Helping students clarify values is a sensitive matter in most situations and precautions must be taken not to become the only professional working with the problem. Professors should become familiar with and have access to the locations of campus offices or governmental agencies with the expertise and authority best able to respond appropriately to student questions about personal problems. Adverse parental reactions, legal ramifications, and students holding professors blameworthy are only a few of the possible negative outcomes of imprudent student advising.

Academic advising with regard to degree programs and other college or university requirements must be handled accurately and honestly. Bad or misleading advice from professors could result in a student going another term or semester, unneeded costs of living and, in some cases, loss of employment opportunities. Professors advising students outside of their area of expertise are putting both students and themselves in jeopardy of future dilemmas. Reliable academic advising is important enough that it must be given top priority. Professors unsure about academic advising simply must become better prepared or advise students where they can go to get the best help available.

Students who *demand confidentiality* as a condition for relating a personal problem are asking professors to compromise their own personal and professional values. If a student says, "I have got to talk with you right now, but you have to promise me you will not tell anyone else," a professional response should be something like, "I cannot promise you confidentiality, but I will promise you that if you choose to tell me your problem, I will do everything I can to help you." Although there may appear to be a fine line between the law and comforting a disillusioned or despondent student, professors must be able to recognize the difference and stay within legal limits and good ethical practice. Emotional involvement is sometimes difficult to avoid, but every effort should be made to maintain a professional relationship. Professors must convince themselves that they are not the only ones that can solve students' personal crises and should solicit the help of the best professionals available.

Whenever possible, professors should take the time and *walk troubled students to the counseling center* on campus and introduce them to someone there who can be of assistance. Just giving them the location and sending them off seldom gets the job done. Everyone who feels troubled needs a clear-thinking friend or professional nearby who cares enough and knows how to help them take the first steps toward getting the assistance they need. Personal problems of students are frequently volatile and fraught with unforeseen repercussions. Empathetic listening is always helpful and highly recommended, but under very few circumstances would faculty ever want to "go it alone" with students who have serious personal problems.

Although the confidential relationship between student and professor is not commonly associated with typical higher education classroom management, unprofessional disclosures by professors often precipitate an attitude of mistrust or resentment on the part of students. On the other hand, professors who show a respect for students' feelings of self-worth and their right to an expectancy of privacy provide the basis for an open and trusting professional relationship. Because of this relationship students will experience a greater sense of security and belonging, which in turn forms the foundation of a successful classroom community.

Complaint Procedures

Casting its shadow over every public rule and decision is the 14th Amendment right of substantive and procedural due process. Whether or not these rights are stated or written, they are implicit in every public institution of higher education's function. How many college or university catalogs or student handbooks, for example, in covering student rights and responsibilities spell out the students' process for appeal concluding with the United States Supreme Court? Frequently the rationale of a professor or an administrator is to accord complaint procedures a low profile in the hope that students will be less likely to complain if they remain uninformed. College and university officials, however, must realize that encouraging student opinion through an accessible and open forum greatly reduces student feelings of frustration, which are often a cause of behavioral problems. For many students, just knowing their opinion will be considered or their grievance heard gives them a positive feeling about the higher education institution and assures them that the college or university has placed a high value on students' rights and interests.

Due process can vary from simply listening to students explain why they were late for class to a formal proceeding involving attorneys, witnesses, and a hearings officer adjudicating findings of fact and conclusions of law. Regardless of the level of the hearing or the expertise of the person conducting it, there are three very important procedural due process aspects essential to a hearing's constitutionality. They are as follows.

(1) *Notice*—an oral or written notice of the charges. In other words, the student has a right to know what rule was violated. For example, "You were cheating on the exam."

(2) *Evidence*—a summary of the evidence against the student. For example, "Your answers were exactly the same as those of the student next to you in the exam room."

(3) *Defense*—an opportunity for the student to be heard. This is simply an opportunity for a student to present his or her side of the story. For example, "We studied together for three nights."

When professors are *"hearing students out"* there is no particular model that must be followed; so any procedure that is fundamentally fair and allows the lawful authority of the institution to be exercised with discretion, and that is not arbitrary or capricious, is satisfactory. In order to meet the test of "fundamentally fair," great emphasis must be placed on interacting with students in a way which does not intimidate or threaten them; they must be treated in a manner that tends to encourage honest and forthright responses.

For example, asking students, "What seems to be the problem?" or even stating the fact, "It looks like we might have a problem," puts students on notice that something is wrong and, at the same time, does not work to stifle good communication. It also allows students to take charge and decide the tone for the conversation. In most cases students know what rule they are violating and often the evidence is quite clear. If not, professors should take the time to clear it up for students in a nonthreatening and helpful sort of way. For example, a student questioning their grade could be given an example of an outstanding paper or essay question written by another student (concealing the name), showing the standard expected for a better grade. Showing students examples gets away from accusations and defensiveness and lets professors get to the issue of what things that student can do now to get their work up to a higher standard. When taking this approach, students generally admit they just did not have the time to study or were ill at the time. When they do this professors can respond by saying, "You must be a genius to be able to do as well as you did with the little effort you put into it." Every time professors will get a smile and note that the conversation will turn toward strategies students can use to change and do things differently next time.

Poor tests and papers are an excellent resource for *diagnostic information* about where students are experiencing trouble with a course. Hearing how complaining students view the situation, making clear to them what is expected, discussing their study habits, suggesting other resources for better understanding, talking about their goals and aspirations, and helping them make contacts with other students in class are only some of the benefits of "due process" interactions with students. Angry or disappointed students bent upon confrontation, who find themselves in the capable hands of a professional educator equally bent upon helping them succeed, will find a "teachable moment" in the conversation that will be long remembered by both. A caring, supportive professor is a powerful motivator to students who need more confidence in themselves and their ability to succeed.

Another problem deals with students who feel more comfortable if they have *someone with them* when talking to a professor about an incident. A request like this should not only be allowed but encouraged. Students accused of wrongdoing should not be made to feel alone in exercising their due process rights. Other students or staff can be very helpful before, during, and after a hearing, not only for their skill and knowledge, but as friends who can assist them processing and dealing with the overall situation. In some instances students from another culture have difficulty understanding our rules or trouble speaking English. In cases such as this a professor should take the time to help those students find someone who is able to represent their interests and interpret for them the institution's way of doing things. Sometimes students will ask their professor to go with them to a hearing across campus that has nothing to do with the professor's class. The professor should regard it as a compliment and go with the student. It is not only a great opportunity to help students, but a real learning experience of how a hearing process feels from the other side. For *major offenses* and serious problems professors should advise students of their right to a formal hearing on the matter that will generally occur at a top administrative level. If there are legal services provided for students on campus, recommend the student contact a lawyer in that office, or if they would feel better about calling home, the family lawyer may be the best source for providing a name of a good attorney in the area. Regardless of a professor's knowledge about due process, they should always counsel students that an attorney is their best source of advice in matters of major importance.

Complaint procedures should be specific about who decides what, on what basis it will be determined, and when it will be resolved. For example, if classroom rules and decisions are discussed first with the professor, and if a satisfactory resolution is not reached, then the appeal process should state the title of the professor's immediate supervisor and the actionable time frames involved. A similar notice of procedure must be followed through to the institution's chief executive officer. From there the appeal is taken to a board governing the institution. The Board is the legal entity of every college or university with final authority for all administrative rules and decisions. If an appeal is denied by the Board, students may appeal to either a federal or state administrative agency or a state or federal trial court, then to an appellate court, and finally, if the justices decide to hear the case, to the United States Supreme Court. To restate it simply, every professor's decision has the possibility of being appealed all the way up to the United States Supreme Court.

It is important to remember that the complaint process works best if each step is played out properly and none are bypassed. For example, if a student complains about a professor to the college or university president, the president should avoid commenting directly on the problem and diplomatically refer the student to the professor's immediate supervisor. Undermining the authority of subordinates is not only a waste of valuable time, but can dampen the team spirit within an organization as well as diminish student respect for the capabilities and authority of "in-the-trenches" professors and their administrators.

The *decision on any appeal* should be decided within a reasonable time period and communicated as soon as possible directly to the parties involved. If at all possible, professors should speak personally with the student. Every effort should be made to be open about the decision and to respond freely and candidly to all questions. If more than one student is interested in an appeal, a conference with all concerned is good administrative practice and has proven to be an effective way to share opinions on sensitive and volatile issues.

Academic and behavioral decisions effecting student liberties and property interests are often placed in the hands of committees. There are problems with this practice. Committees or student courts are not very effective at getting to the source of student problems or enabling them to change their attitudes. The professional student/professor relationship and judicious consequences are specifically designed for that purpose and far better oriented to helping students resolve problems in a confidential and personalized relationship. Students are more likely to open up and talk about their personal feelings to their professors and advisors than to a committee of their peers. However, many colleges have decided to use student committees and courts to mete out appropriate punishments to students who violate the rules. In this case, students who serve on appeals committees must be cautioned about the importance of confidentiality and the problems associated with bias, stereotyping private lifestyles of other students, and peer pressure to gossip or be swayed in making equitable and fair decisions. Because of the importance to the future opportunities of students, student appeals committees should be adequately prepared and properly briefed about the considerable responsibility of deciding on the property and liberty interests of others.

A balance must be maintained between the students' rights to adequate notice, a fair hearing, and appeal, with the institution of higher education's need for the orderly and efficient operation of its educational mission. Time taken to implement due process procedures sometimes seems to distract from other educational and administrative responsibilities. However, in the long run, the rewards for respecting and teaching students' due process rights are endless, for the students as well as the college or university. It is our sincere hope that *The Judicious Professor* may be a moving force behind a positive student/professor relationship; effusive enough to give an impetus to modeling at least three of our nation's highest moral and cultural values — freedom, justice, and equality.

Chapter Seven

Judicious Prudence: Ideology and Politics

The previous chapters have presented an incipient philosophy for professors who aspire to establish and maintain a learner-centered approach for teaching and learning in higher education. Chapter One introduced the philosophy as a dialogic approach to teaching and learning and discussed this approach's affect on student perceptions of professors as professionals and we presented ethical considerations that positively and negatively impact the professional posture of professors. We argued that *The Judicious Professor* will have a positive influence on students when acting in ways that complement the ethics of the profession of teaching and when never doing things that may well jeopardize a healthy student/professor relationship. For the most part it is what the professor never does that helps to maintain a viable teaching and learning relationship.

Chapter Two articulated learning theory that professors need to know about in order to meet the educational needs of all students. In Chapter Three we presented a constitutional perspective as a complementary rationale for maintaining a judicious teaching and learning relationship within a democratic classroom environment. We demonstrated in Chapter Four how professors and students can establish and maintain mutual goals and expectations and use them to guide teaching and learning relationships in college and university courses and beyond, as we know a viable teaching and learning relationship invariably lasts a lifetime.

Chapter Five spoke to the need for judicious professors to maintain professional teaching and learning relationships with students even when mutual goals and expectations have been strained or broken by student conduct or inaction. We revealed a professional mind-set for dealing with students in problematic situations and cited examples professors might use to help students recover, while still maintaining a viable professional relationship.

Chapter Six conveyed a synthesis and evaluation of student constitutional rights, good educational practice, and professional ethics counterbalanced with the problems and practical realities of classroom leadership. In Appendix I we will argue how the biology of learning demands a judicious philosophy when teaching and learning in higher education. Appendix II provides instrumentation and web-based resources for self-evaluating the effective implementation of mutual goals and expectations and the establishment of mutual respect with whole classes of students through pretesting and posttesting students for stages of social development.

The Judicious Professor *and Ideology*

The Judicious Professor provides reason and language for a civil ideology, based on mutual respect and trust. This is made manifest in a professor's professional ethics, respect for principles of cognitive psychology, and sound educational practice, legal precedence, and the biology of learning.

One aspect of an ideology is that it provides schemata, or conceptual and political maps of social reality, that are individually applied as a result of social or psychological strain. Schemata are socially constructed, and so it follows that when students enter the classroom, they bring with them many different ideas and expectations about teaching and learning. *The Judicious Professor* works to develop a "collective conscience" among students with mutually agreed upon goals and expectations that mark the borders and pathways of social acceptability in the teaching and learning environment, e.g., students and professor may agree that it is reasonable to assume that they will listen to each other.

Language and Politics

There is great power in language. Language is not simply a conduit for communication; it is the DNA of schema. Schemata are encoded in a language framework that determines the political process for activation and application. As a result, it is impossible to think about language without thinking about power and politics. Schemata are metaphorically constructed with language and encoded and embedded in previous ways of knowing. They emanate from culture and traditions; and these previous ways of knowing are embedded in metaphors, as well, e.g., in traditional higher education we often hear metaphors like, "the test was a breeze" or "scholarship is publication."

Metaphors are transmitted through language and thus, templates of culture and tradition are augmented and changed as the language use and application changes. In this way, language controls ideology and schema development. It is through language and the lack of language, creating areas of silence, that culture and tradition are maintained. But, as a result of changing language, culture and tradition are always in a state of dynamic disequilibrium or constant change and adaptation. The politics of constructing conceptual maps or schemata through language and metaphor ensure that culture is never static; and it is the purpose of this book to help professors take responsibility for determining the direction of cultural change through teaching about and using the *language of civility* in their teaching and learning relationships.

Language will both facilitate and hide political interests, e.g., a monological approach creates areas of silence that hide democracy, whereas a dialogical approach advances democracy and mutual respect. There is great political and economic power invested in those who control the language and the channels of communication. For this reason, institutions of higher education have traditionally guarded the language used in classrooms and the channels of communication permitted individuals. *The Judicious Professor* challenges traditional channels of communication and authoritative language by empowering the professor and students with a *language of civility* and a learner-centered philosophy for teaching and learning. It uses the power of language as a change agent that is actively involved in the construction of reality and a shared consciousness that we call a culture of civility.

Since all ideologies are "front-loading," professors must first teach students about the *language of civility* and give them examples and opportunities to make decisions based on principles embedded in the language. It is unreasonable for professors to think that students can and will operate at the higher levels of consciousness simply by entering the classroom. Students need to be taught the language of civility and provided with models for applying that language to problematic situations. And, should students find themselves in those situations, they need professors who can model appropriate knowledge, dispositions, and skills at a principled level and who can help them to recover and realign with the class culture. Implementing this philosophy in hopes of establishing a civil culture, semester after semester, has more to do with the professor than with the students who enter the classroom.

The Judicious Professor is actively involved in constructing a culture of mutual respect and trust between the professor and every student in the college or university. This philosophy will only work well in classrooms where professors and students alike are actively involved in establishing mutual expectations and goals, with guidance and reason from the professor which is balanced with the input of ideas from students, and when everyone in the classroom agrees to be an active participant in establishing the class culture.

Context Is Everything

Finally, we offer a word of caution and hope. *The Judicious Professor* could be perceived in dichotomous ways: as a threat to the more traditional practices in higher education, or as a positive force among colleagues. The authors hope that it will be the latter, and that this book will help colleagues develop an awareness of what a dialogical approach to teaching and learning, within a democratic culture, can do to enhance and maintain mutual respect and trust between students and their professors. Judicious professors, guided by universal principles of civility, and operating at the highest level of awareness, need to be mindful of the effect their "professionalism" is having on colleagues and administrators who only know and use a monological approach.

As Langer (1989) reminds us in her book, *Mindfulness*, "Our perceptions and interpretations influence the way our bodies respond. *When the 'mind' is in a context, the 'body' is necessarily also in that context.* To achieve a different physiological state, sometimes what we need to do is to place the mind in another context" (p. 177). *The Judicious Professor* can help everyone construct a mind-set and thus a physiological context that emphasizes mutual respect and responsibility in the teaching and learning relationship.

In this context, students will quickly know that things are "different" when they come in contact with *The Judicious Professor*. Generally their reaction is one of enthusiasm and gratitude. As one student remarked on her signed course evaluation, "I appreciated the fact that I could get my papers in late, with no grade penalty, but I always got them in on time out of respect." The simple act of providing a schedule indicating when assignments are due, but allowing students to submit their work when they have had an opportunity to do their best work, conveys a respect for the student's learning that is returned to the professor. With mutual respect in place, the teaching and learning relationship moves to a higher level of trust while maintaining the same academic rigor.

When professors make that paradigm shift, that philosophical and cognitive leap to *The Judicious Professor*, they feel confident and at ease every time a student calls out for help ... "Professor!"

Appendix I

The Brain and Cognition, Affect, and Behavior

The one organ in the human body that professors deal with most in their work is the human brain. However, as an association of professionals, professors generally know very little about the brain and how it works. Developing some fundamental understandings about how the brain holistically constructs a mentality and a propensity for action provides professors with more tools and approaches for meeting the individual needs of every student. Gaining understanding about the human brain provides professors with some clues to assist them in their work as mentors and curriculum associates in the learning process.

It is understandable that professors would have so little knowledge of the brain. The human brain is the most complicated organ in the body and knowledge about the brain and how it works is advancing rapidly. However, it is important for professors to keep up with recent studies in the area of neuroscience and cognitive psychology. Current thinking has great significance for education and learning, and new developments continue to challenge the wisdom of popular educational practices.

The Developing Brain

It was thought that every individual was endowed, at birth, with the full complement of brain cells (neurons) she or he would enjoy for the rest of his/her life and that the maximum number and configuration of brain cells was normally "fixed" at the moment of conception and no one could generate new brain cells after birth. Recent research suggests this is probably not true. However, the number of functional brain cells will vary from person to person, i.e., we are not all given the same number of brain cells and this is a result of environmental and genetic circumstances. A "normal" human brain is endowed with approximately one hundred billion functional brain cells (Kandel, Schwartz & Jessell, 1991). Figure 1 displays a typical brain cell or neuron.

"The role of a neuron is to receive information from outside and to transmit through its three fundamental parts: the cell body, the dendrites, and the axon" (Levinthal, 1988, p. 54). It is the job of the cell body and dendrites to take in information from other nerve cells. It is the job of the axon to pass that information on to other brain cells.

In a normal brain, neurons are specialized and systematically organized in ways that allow individuals to, at once, process complex tasks of perception, thought, and action (Damasio, 1994; Holloway, 1992).

Neurons are not haphazardly arranged. The neurons organize into interconnected systems or neurological pathways by

---

Figure 1.

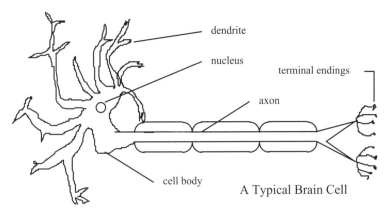

dendrite

nucleus

terminal endings

axon

cell body   A Typical Brain Cell

three important "architects" and "construction workers" who "build" the brain. These three architects and builders are: *genetics* (the coding of biological information on DNA), *experience* (any physical and/or perceived interaction between an individual and the environment), and *metaphorical imagination* (the linking of new thoughts and feelings to the known). These three (genetics, experience, and metaphorical imagination), work collaboratively to construct a *mentality* and a *propensity for action* that is historically founded in *culture*.

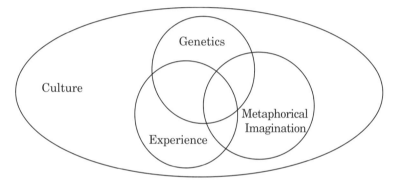

Within an individual's culture, these three architects and construction workers act in concert, in a holistic and life-long interplay of neurological and biochemical cause and effect relationships.

However, each architect/construction worker has a primary role to play in building a brain's intellectual, physical, and emotional capabilities. The primary role for *genetics* is to accurately develop and maintain the neuronal systems (integrated neurophysiology) and concomitant biochemistry. The primary role for *experience* is to prune functional brain cells that are of little use to the individual and identify functional brain cells that are of most use and maximize their potential. The primary role for *metaphorical imagination* is to nurture the functional brain cells that are of most use to the individual and help them to make new connections with other functional brain cells, thereby setting up new neural pathways. In concert, within their own role and specialized function, all three architect/construction workers are responsible for the release and synthesis of biochemicals in the brain. The primary role of *culture* is to provide the context within which all three architect/construction workers can build. To carry through on the metaphor of "building a brain," the primary role and function of culture is that of the zoning commission. *Culture* determines what will be built and what will not be built by comparing the potential a brain has for development and the environmental circumstances surrounding the individual brain. *Culture* helps to maintain and encode the history and ideology of an individual's ancestors in the brain.

By discussing a newborn child's capacity for language acquisition we can examine the primary roles of the three architect/construction workers and the importance of *culture* in providing context. First, *genetics* endows all "normal" newborn children with the ability to acquire and socially use all the languages of the world, complete with the appropriate phonemic intonations. By the first year of life, unless children have been exposed to language and phonemes outside their own culture, children are able to operate best within their own culturally specific language framework, e.g., American English, Japanese, or Chinese.

Second, because of *culturally specific experience* and exposure to language, every normal child will be deprived of alternative language acquisition strategies, due to neurological pruning. While investigating phonemic recognition, McAuliffe (1985) found that babies from birth to six months can recognize every sound imaginable. Yet, after six months babies lose the ability to recognize sounds that are not used in their immediate environment. It is thought that the neurological connections responsible for recognition of little used phonemes are irretrievably destroyed by an enzyme called "calpain."

Third, after the age of one, children can still approximate language acquisition through *metaphorical imagination*, which nurtures the connections between functional brain cells and makes new neural pathways for phonemic recognition and voice synthesis. "When a neuron in the brain dies (and about 10,000 of them apparently do each day), there may be some 'sprouting' of axon terminals of adjacent neurons, but there is always a net loss" (Levinthal, 1988, p. 55).

Fourth, this all occurs within *culture*, an assimilated *culture* that determines the extent to which language will be acquired and used. For example, Asian students learning English as a second language often have difficulty pronouncing the "r" sound. *Culture* determines early in life that many individuals born in Asian countries are not exposed to the "r" phoneme. As a result, the other three architects and construction workers building the brain make it physically difficult, if not immediately impossible, to pronounce the English word "rice."

On a more personal note, as a native-born Oregonian, one of the authors lived for fourteen years in Australia and never acquired a "proper" Australian accent. The neurons for phonemic recognition and voice synthesis were just not present in the brain, and because of *culture*, the brain simply does not miss what is not there. The author didn't even notice that he had a "speech impediment"; he thought he was a "normal" Australian until he was made aware of this neurological condition by one of "his best mates" just before leaving Australia to reside again in the United States. A couple of hours before he was to board the plane to return to the United States, his good mate, Barry, informed him that for the last fourteen years he had been mispronouncing his name. He said, "What, Berry?" Barry said, "Yeah, you always pronounce my name "Berry," which is something you eat, instead of "Barry," which is my name."

Needless to say, the author was embarrassed and tried to reconcile his mistake by pronouncing Barry's name correctly, with the proper Australian intonation. Yet, try as best he could, he was unable to produce the proper bleating "a" sound that is followed quickly by a soft "r" sound. The experience was incredibly frustrating as he repeatedly tried to pronounce Barry's name "properly." After working for quite some time, the two mates finally compromised. They decided that from that time on the author would refer to Barry as, "Bazza," which is the Aussie nickname for "Barry." It appears that the author had no trouble at all finding the proper "a" sound when it was followed by a buzzing "z" sound. The neuronal connections seemed to be in tact for that language task.

In the good news/bad news scenario, the bad news is we're *genetically* given a limited number of brain cells at birth and those neurons are systematically "weeded out" by *experience*. But, the good news is, the remaining functional brain cells are *not* "hard wired," and every individual's *genetics, experience,* and *metaphorical imaginings* work to help neurons change shape and form new connections between other functioning brain cells and new research indicates that we may be able to generate new brain cells. As a result of this ongoing activity, every individual's *genetics, experience,* and *metaphorical imaginings* are constantly engaged in planning and redesigning the brain's shape and biochemistry, *within the context of culture.*

Historically, educational practices have evolved around metaphors of the brain as a vessel to be filled with knowledge, or as a sponge that mops up information, and more recently, as a computer. However, the human brain exhibits a plasticity that confounds such metaphors of thinking about the brain. Today, we know the shape, and biochemical makeup of the brain, is *physically changed* by *experience* and *metaphorical imagination.* We know that such physical change is fueled by a *genetically* determined capacity for memory and perception. As a result, this knowledge invites new and more powerful metaphors for describing and thinking about the brain and teaching and learning. The brain is "plastic," and it is "wet," with balanced states of biochemical activity.

Professors who adopt metaphors of the brain that embrace notions of neural plasticity and a need for biochemical balance can find hope in the belief that every student has the ability to construct a mentality and a propensity for action that falls within the realm of social and cultural acceptability. These will be our learner-centered professors. These professors use their knowledge of the brain to mentor students with a hope for realigning and nurturing neural pathways and biochemical activities and guide students toward pro-social thoughts and actions. These are the professors who will use time and educational strategies to make a difference in the lives of their students.

It is nearly incomprehensible to think that a typical neuron may have as many as one thousand connections with other neurons and that a normal brain typically has 100 billion neurons. When considering all the biochemical messengers in the brain as well as the number of possible connections, this equates the approximate number of possible neuronal connections in a normal brain to be near infinite (Levinthal, 1988). The implications of this potential for brain development and teaching and learning are awesome and should provide all educators with great hope for every individual. We need never give up hope.

Emotion, Cognition, and Body Are Inextricably Linked

Still another common misconception among professors is the idea that the brain is only about thinking or cognition and that pure thought or rationality has little to do with the psycho-motor or the affective domains. In his book, *Descartes' Error*, Antonio R. Damasio (1994) provides thought-provoking arguments and empirical reasoning to support the human brain as a center for a holistic interplay between the cognitive, affective, and psychomotor domains. He provides compelling support for the idea that we construct a mentality and that mentality is based on all that the brain and body do. Ostensibly, he suggests that emotion, thought, and the physical body are all intrinsically linked, one affecting the other in a cascade of biochemical and neurological activity.

Damasio's research supports the existence of a somatic marker system or acquired "gut feeling" in normal individuals that is based on emotion and body awareness and is essential for successful social living and pro-social decision-making. He proposes that somatic markers or "gut feelings" are acquired emotional overtones that mediate our rational thought processes. "Somatic markers are thus acquired by experience, under the control of an internal preference system, and under the influence of an external set of circumstances that include not only entities and events with which the individual must interact, but also social conventions and ethical rules" (Damasio, p. 179). Damasio points out that some people do not have the ability to learn or pay attention to a somatic marker system. He indicates that these are the exceptions and they are not "normal." For example, trauma patients with damage to the left anterior frontal lobe of the brain have lost the ability to establish somatic markers as a result of their traumatic experience. As well, he points out that psychopaths and sociopaths do not seem to experience the full range of feelings of guilt or remorse for their antisocial actions. People such as these, who are not "normal," tend to live their lives as a disaster. These people make poor life decisions with disastrous effects on themselves and the world around them.

Somatic markers or "gut feelings" are linked to various events in our lives, whether real or imagined, and they are metaphorically transferred to new situations. In this way, they assist cognitive processing by providing an emotional overtone when attending to the perceived consequences of a planned action. For example, we can experience negative gut feelings when contemplating decisions and actions that run a risk to our own health and safety. In other words, running in a crowded hallway may not be the best way to move from A to B, or going skydiving without proper instruction is probably not the best choice for recreational activity. As well, we can experience positive gut feelings that are based on notions of delayed gratification; for example, doing "hard work" in class or cleaning up the science experiment. These actions may be associated with positive gut feelings based on delayed gratification, linked to perceived payment of future dividends for "good" behavior. Or, the actions may be linked to altruism. This appendix will argue that it is in the best interests of the student and the rest of society that institutions of higher education and professors should emphasize altruism, rather than material rewards, as a basis for social decision-making.

Somatic markers or "gut feelings" are also linked to "Sign Stimulus." A sign stimulus is a visual, kinesthetic, and/or auditory signal that activates a predetermined mental and emotional state in the individual. Every individual perceives a sign stimulus differently and the same sign stimulus may activate different "gut feelings" in different individuals (Damasio, 1994). For example, the words "pop quiz" may signal a "gut feeling" of heightened anxiety for the ill prepared student and a "gut feeling" of jubilation for the well-prepared student. Often a "stereotypical response" is the first proposition considered by an individual when a sign stimulus activates an individual somatic marker. A "stereotypical response" is characterized by a consist pattern of behavior that occurs in virtually the same order and fashion every time. Using the "pop quiz" example, an ill prepared student, upon hearing the words "pop quiz" from the professor, may experience an unpleasant "gut feeling" and tacitly activate a series of idiosyncratic avoidance behaviors. A colleague of ours tells a story about her seventh-grade biology teacher who used to ask questions of the class and then call on students whether they raised their hands or not. If a student didn't know the answer, the teacher would voice some demeaning comment that embarrassed the student. By coincidence, our colleague discovered that if she were in the act of blowing her nose the teacher would never call on her. So, she developed a somatic marker and a stereotypical response to alleviate the situation. Whenever her biology teacher began asking questions (her sign stimulus) a negative gut feeling came over her (her somatic marker) and she immediately reached for her box of tissues and blew her nose (her stereotypical response). The teacher never called on her.

Brain Plasticity and the Effect of Culture

The brain's capacity and capability for perception and memory are the keys to cognitive processing. Our students, literally, physically construct a personal "reality" by dynamically building biochemical and physical dendrite connections between neurons. Students' experiences and metaphorical imaginings generate new dendrite "spines" and axon terminals (nerve endings) which reach out and make new neuronal connections.

...synaptic change [or brain plasticity] is a sum of moment-to-moment changes laid successively upon each other. In this way each new moment of experience adds to, or subtracts from, whatever has just preceded. At any particular moment, the pattern of synaptic change provides a running average of what has occurred previously. (Squire, 1987, p. 240)

This neuronal adaptation is a "dynamic" process where experience and metaphorical imagination generate new neuron connections, which proposes and invites behavior and interaction with the environment, that when acted upon results in new experience and metaphorical imagination, that forms new neuron connections. It continues in a "genetic" cycle of behavior/ experience within culture/metaphorical imagination/genetic coding/behavior/ and on it goes... (Bachevalier, 1990; Edelman, 1987; Ornstein & Thompson, 1984).

A student's brain is always physically adapting to new input and redefining behavior thought appropriate for a situation, which is reflected in the student's ever-changing ideas, beliefs, attitudes, and values. Professors need to realize and understand that students always act in ways they think are in their best interests. Students simply do the best they can with what they are given. It is normal for students to physically construct neuronal circuits with balanced states of biochemical and neuro-electrical activity; and these balanced states become their conceptual maps of social reality and cultural ways of knowing; these are their schemata.

Schemata are constructed as a result of socialization inside culture. This is the work of education. If we broadly define culture as the sum of ways of living built up by a group of human beings, which is transmitted from one generation to another, it is relatively safe to say that very little is learned outside culture, in fact it is difficult to think of anything outside this definition of culture. Hence, the culture we live in and learn in is very important. From the day we are conceived, the quality of the culture we are born into will do much to help determine our future freedoms and liberty. Remember the example cited earlier indicating how a child born into a culture rich in a wide range of phonemes was better able to enhance and strengthen neurological connections associated with properly acquiring and using the language of the culture. Well, it is also possible that from an early age a sense of others and attitudes concomitant with pro-social activity can be transmitted via a caring culture and that these modal values can be embedded in an individual as somatic markers.

> The automated somatic-marker device of most of us lucky enough to have been reared in a relatively healthy culture has been accommodated by education to the standards of rationality of that culture. In spite of its roots in biological regulation, the device has been tuned to cultural prescriptions designed to ensure survival in a particular society. If we assume that the brain is normal and the culture in which it develops is healthy, the device has been made rational relative to social conventions and ethics. (Damasio, 1994, p. 200)

The need for a healthy culture is very important in the early years of life, and because of our capability for neural plasticity, a healthy culture is important throughout a lifetime.

The Importance
of a Healthy Culture for Learning

There is a need to create a healthy classroom culture that is based on principles of civility and that supports learning by teaching and endorsing socially acceptable thoughts, emotions, and behaviors. A healthy classroom culture cannot be based on rewards and punishment; it must operate at the principled level of moral development. It must consider the cognitive, affective, and psycho-motor domains as holistically integrated and equally important. Only when the classroom culture acknowledges the holistic interplay of all three domains and operates at the principled level will the culture empower students with automated somatic markers that can be transferred from social situation to social situation. Only when students view the classroom as a safe and caring environment in which to live and learn will they learn to take the calculated risks and take responsibility for their own social action.

A classroom culture that is based on rewards and punishment will not offer students consistent opportunities to transfer social skills, because students will tend to view each social situation as an isolated instance in learning. In other words, there is no consistency in time, place, and manner. Every social action is rewarded or punished by those in authority and whether the student is rewarded or punished is simply based upon idiosyncratic criteria. Students then acquire bits of information, but are not afforded the "grand picture." For example, professor "A" marks students tardy if they are not in their seats one second after the bell rings and professor "B" allows students all the time they need to make it to class. When rewards and punishments are meted out by professors, and they stem from unilateral professor-centered decisions, students learn to obey the professor; they do not become responsible learners. A rewards and punishment culture encourages codependency and obedience by the student. Students who view their classrooms as limiting and restrictive environments in which to live and learn are less likely to take responsibility for their social actions; they will simply learn to be obedient to certain authorities in a specific time, place, and manner.

Students activate specific neuronal circuits or schemata in response to a personally constructed perception of their environment, which is mediated by their learning within culture. The perceived environment may be "real" or "imaginary"; perception is personal. To illustrate this point, consider this simple experiment. When asked about who first signed the Declaration of Independence, in big handwriting, many people schooled in the continental United States respond with the name "John Hancock." This fact is generally taught in fifth-grade social studies classes across the United States. John Hancock was the first person to sign the Declaration of Independence and he wrote his signature in big handwriting so the King of England would not have to wear his "spectacles" in order to read his signature. In fact, this story has become so much a part of continental United States culture that many people living in the continental United States tacitly expect others to know what they mean when they ask them to "put their John Hancock right there." It is expected that the person will hand write their signature on a piece of paper.

To conduct the experiment, ask someone who was schooled in the continental United States, "Who was the first person to write his signature on the Declaration of Independence?" After the person responds "John Hancock," ask this question, "What is a key signature?" Generally the person will be dumbfounded and unable to respond. Ask them to think about it, "What is a key signature?" Is John Hancock's signing of the Declaration of Independence a key signature? Is the signing of any legal document a key signature? Many people will be puzzled by this question because the neuronal circuits, or schema, responsible for knowledge about the "signing process," the schema of peoples' signatures, have been activated by the previous question about the signing of the Declaration of Independence. However, when the word "music" is mentioned, a whole new set of neuronal circuits (new schemata) are activated in the person's brain and this provides him or her with a new "environmental and/or cultural context"; and thus a new meaning for the term "Key Signature" can emerge. If the person possesses knowledge of music, she or he will probably respond, "A key signature is a group of sharps or flats to the right of the clef sign on a musical staff."

This illustrates the importance of perception and cultural context in providing rational responses to problematic situations. Consider those students who perceive the environment as a limiting and restrictive place to live and how they will constantly activate schemata that are dramatically different from the schemata activated by students who perceive their environment as free and caring. A student's perception of her or his environment is important in determining how she or he will behave and learn.

All Learning Is Biological

As fantastic as it seems, the sophisticated thinking processes and concomitant cultural ways of knowing fabricated by every individual have microscopic origins. The ultimate unit of action in the brain and in the process of "knowing" is a biochemical messenger called a *neurotransmitter*. Neurotransmitters are molecular structures that relay information from one neuron to another. "If ... neurons are the processors of information, then the brain chemicals [neurotransmitters] are the languages through which information processing is carried out" (Levinthal, 1988, p. 53).

Communication between brain cells occurs when stored neurotransmitters in one brain cell are released from the axon terminals (nerve endings). They move across a synaptic gap (a space between neurons as neurons never touch each other) and attach themselves to specific neurotransmitter receptors on the dendrites (receiving cables) and cell body of the receiving neuron. The communication effect that neurotransmitters have on the receiving neuron is either to excite or inhibit the receiving neuron, depending upon the receiving neuron's electro-chemical alignment. Every neuron has an electric charge across its membrane; a charge of about one tenth of a volt, positive on the outside and negative on the inside. When a neuron is excited by neurotransmitters, it "fires" by reversing the polarity of the electrical charge from the outside to the inside of the neuron, sending a "nerve impulse" in a wave from the cell body, down the axon, to the terminal endings. "Exciting" the neuron occurs when enough neurotransmitters attach themselves to the receptors on the dendrites and cell body to amass a critical threshold, bioelectrically. The receiving neuron then opens sodium gates in the axon, beginning nearest the cell body, and allows a cascade of positively charged sodium ions to rush inside the axon and open other sodium channel gates further down the axon as the positive charge moves toward the terminal endings in the dendrites. When the electrical charge finally reaches the terminal ending, biochemicals are released into the synaptic space between neurons to communicate with the next neurons, and so forth and so on. This process all occurs in milliseconds.

It takes the neuron about a thousandth of a second to recover, reinstating itself back to a "resting state" after "firing." Then, it can "fire" again. When repeatedly "excited," it is possible for neurons to "fire" thousands of times per second or they may "fire"

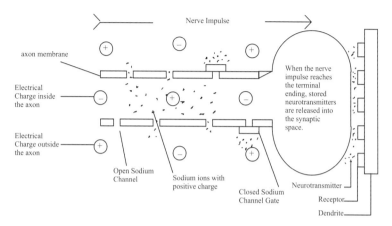

just a few times every second; and some neurons, that are "inhibited" by biochemical activity, simply remain in a "resting state" and do not fire at all.

Neurotransmitters communicate with other neurons by making the nerve cell "more" or "less" likely to "fire." Neurotransmitters tend to inhibit communication between neurons when the message they carry affects the electrical charge of the receiving neuron by opening chloride channels in the cell body. This allows negatively charged chloride ions to enter the cell body of the neuron. The chloride ions make the brain cell more negatively charged on the inside. As a result, the surrounding biochemicals and neurotransmitters binding to the receptors on the dendrites of the neuron must overcome a greater negative electronic charge, or threshold, before the neuron can "fire." The greater the number of chloride ions, the greater the negative charge in the neuron or the greater the threshold, and the less likely it is to pass the message on to the next neuron by "firing" or activating a "nerve impulse" (Ornstein & Thompson, 1984).

A brain cell's firing or "nerve impulse" is an all or nothing process. It is a change in the electrical charge of a neuron. A nerve impulse is always the same; it either "fires" or there is nothing and the nerve cell remains in a "resting state." The only variable during a nerve impulse is the speed at which the nerve impulse travels down the axon to the terminal endings. Some neurons take more *time* to pass the message on to other neurons, because they simply do not "fire" very fast or very often. The speed at which any given neuron "fires" can vary from one kilometer per hour to two hundred kilometers per hour. The speed with which neurons "fire" is measured in time; so time is important in the teaching and learning process.

Unlike the nerve impulse, the synaptic transmission of neurotransmitters is a "graded" form of communication. Any given neuron, for a variety of reasons, could release huge numbers of neurotransmitters into the synaptic space or relatively few. The graded communication occurs because the more neurotransmitters released and the greater the receptivity of the dendrites receptors, the better the chances for exciting the next neuron and causing it to "fire."

Both the "all or nothing" nerve impulse and the "graded" neurotransmitter release are needed to transfer biological information from one brain cell to the next (Kandel, *et al.*, 1991; Levinthal, 1990; Ornstein & Thompson, 1984). It is through this incredible act of neuronal communication, multiplied billions of times, that human beings perpetuate a "genetic" cycle of learning which consists of genetic coding, experience within culture and metaphorical imagination, behavior, and biochemical and neuronal adaptation.

The Genetic Cycle of Learning

The term "genetic" cycle of learning is used in this appendix as both a figure of speech and a literal interpretation. As a figure of speech, "genetic" infers a learning cycle that feeds on itself, whose "genesis" is manifest in its past and whose future is dependent upon the present action, reaction, or inaction. As a literal interpretation, "genetic" refers to a neurological process where neurotransmitters affect the "genetic coding" within brain cells. This literal interpretation is articulated by Kandel, *et al.* (1991) as they discuss the relationship between genes and behavior:

Genes are essential not only for producing the appropriate neural circuitry of a behavior, but also for regulating the expression of the behavior in the adult, because genes code the structural proteins necessary to maintain the neuronal circuitry as well as for enzymes—including the transmitter-synthesizing enzymes that are essential for normal synaptic transmission. Moreover, genes directly code for peptide hormones and modulators that trigger or inhibit the expression of behavior. (p. 992)

This suggests that there is a link between genes and behavior, and it is a complex relationship. Professors must work with a multiplicity of individual personalities and learning styles in classrooms daily. Good professors know that every individual is different. For years biology courses have taught about these differences through knowledge of human conception and the probabilities of inheriting different physical characteristics from parents. These courses teach that when the egg is fertilized, information is coded on genes and that many of the approximately one hundred thousand genes will dictate an individual's physical characteristics. What is not generally taught, is that along with the genes that ultimately determine an individual's physical characteristics (male/female, fair/dark skin), there is also a set of genes that determine certain "personality characteristics" (Restak, 1994).

Students come to the classroom with a propensity for action, thought, and feeling, much of which is genetically inherited from their parents in the same way they inherit their physical attributes.

...Dr. Frank A. Elliott, professor Emeritus of Neurology at the University of Pennsylvania School of Medicine...has spent a lifetime studying violent people, [and] is convinced that genetic inheritance is one of the biological factors influencing the capacity for aggression. This capacity is mediated by a system of neurons and neurotransmitters extending from the prefrontal cortex down to the lower brain stem. "Most of this equipment is situated in the deep central portions of the brain which we have inherited, almost unchanged, from our reptilian and early mammalian ancestors," says Elliott. Experiments have made it clear that electrical stimulation of key sites along this pathway within the limbic system can provoke angry aggressive behavior or childhood predatory attacks. (Restak, 1988, p. 283)

As will be more thoroughly discussed later, it is logical to think that individual students can inherit a propensity for aggression through a genetically acquired deficiency in neurotransmitters (serotonin levels) that leads to impulsive, injurious aggression and a reduced self-esteem.

Not only intelligence but such personality factors as shyness, introversion, and susceptibility to certain forms of mental illness are turning out to be heavily influenced by genetics. This does not at all portend a gloomy determinism; life experiences can sometimes modify the basic personality, even transform it into its opposite. (Restak, 1994, p.99)

Personalities can be changed; our students do not have "solid state" neuronal circuits and set levels of biochemical activity. Students can alter their personalities by "cultivating" new nerve endings (dendrites and axon terminals) that "grow" and reach out to communicate with other neurons; and remember, the number of possible connections in a normal human brain are virtually limitless (Kandel, et al., 1991; Restak, 1988; Squire, 1987).

Phosphorylation is one neurological process that can affect a brain cell's genetic code (Kandel, 1994). It is a complicated process that is best described by beginning at the end and working backwards to its origin. Genes are coded by "...various combinations of the twenty amino acids and four nucleotides that make up our proteins" (Restak, 1994, p. 99). These proteins make the individual what he or she is mentally, physically, and emotionally. Some genes have two segments on which proteins arrange themselves in a genetic code. One segment is the message and the other determines whether the gene will be "read or transcribed," i.e., whether the gene will be eligible for action. This second region of genetic coding activates or deactivates the gene by the binding of specific proteins. Only genes that have a particular characteristic, called *cyclic AMP recognition element*, can be switched on and off by the binding of proteins. Not every gene in the body has this "switching characteristic." There are thousands of genes that will never be affected and these are the genes determining hair color, skin color and the color of our eyes; these genes will never be affected by "normal processes." But, there are also thousands of genes that can be turned on and off by a *cyclic AMP recognition element binding protein*. When genes are turned on and off by this neurological process we literally change the genetic code of the brain cell. It is thought that specific genes are "turned on" to produce the proteins that are essential for learning and long term memory. Kandel, *et. al.* (1991) have found that learning and long term memory *require* protein synthesis and changes in genetic coding at the cellular level.

The Importance of Serotonin in Learning and Long-Term Memory

One of the primary neurotransmitters involved in phosphorylation and essential for learning and memory is serotonin. Serotonin strengthens the synaptic connections between nerve cells involved in learning and memory by activating secondary messengers that phosphorylate proteins within the cell. When Serotonin binds to a brain cell's receptor, one of the things it can do is activate an enzyme called adenylyl cyclase. This enzyme converts a molecule that powers the brain cell, ATP, to a secondary intracellular messenger, cyclic AMP. Cyclic AMP activates another enzyme, a protein kinase, which adds phosphate groups to other proteins. This phosphorylation of proteins increases or decreases the activity of the proteins (Kandel & Hawkins, 1992). In other words, it switches the proteins "on" or "off." If serotonin is repeatedly applied to the same brain cell, protein kinases not only act on the proteins within the cytoplasm of the cell, but they will also act on genes within the nucleus. The serotonin induced protein kinases will also affect the genes that give rise to neuronal growth and the genes that make the kinases persistently active even in the absence of cyclic AMP (Kandel, 1994). So, what does all this mean to the average professor? *Serotonin is absolutely essential for learning and memory* (Kandel, 1994). Without this neurotransmitter students will learn nothing, because they will retain nothing! This means that serotonin is involved in all aspects of cognition and behavior.

Serotonin is not only essential for learning and memory; it is also involved with mediating self-esteem and social behavior. One of its roles is to inhibit aggressive behavior. Raleigh and Brammer (1993) found that monkeys displaying social behavior that is well aligned with group expectations tend to have greater serotonin activity and greater numbers of serotonin-2 receptors in the specific areas of the brain that are concerned with social behavior than do monkeys who display antisocial aggressive behavior. They also found that when serotonin activity was blocked in the more social monkeys, they were more likely to display impulsive, injurious aggression. "In general, enhancing serotonin function reduces aggression and favors social behavior" (Damasio, 1994, p. 76).

It is simply fascinating to think that serotonin is linked to both feelings of self-worth and social behavior, and at the same time to learning and memory. Experienced professors have tacitly known for years that students who have high self-esteem and tend to be intrinsically motivated to act in socially appropriate ways are more likely to learn and apply the knowledge, dispositions, and skills taught in the various academic disciplines. These students also tend to be more involved in extracurricular activities than those students who feel inadequate and are denied perceptions of self-worth. The implications for professors and strategies for teaching and learning are clear. Serotonin is a biochemical link between behavior, cognition, and feelings of self-worth. The appropriate educational response is for professors to set up and promote a classroom culture that gives students feelings of permanent value; provide a classroom where students do not need to prove themselves in order to fit in with the social group and the learning community. This, in turn, helps to raise students' levels of serotonin, improving social interaction and learning and memory. A healthy classroom culture helps to develop the neuronal circuits and biochemistry needed to be a viable and healthy human being.

Still, some will argue that a better avenue and a quicker solution for those lacking in socially appropriate behaviors is found by using drugs to complement an individual's physical need for greater serotonin activity. Certainly drugs, like Prozac, have a role to play in realigning some students' behavior with the social norms and expectations for proper schooling. However, prescription drugs should be a last resort as there is always a danger associated with applying a "shot gun" technique to a problem that needs "pin-point" accuracy. For example, Prozac is often prescribed for depression and it acts to "clog" the reuptake of serotonin from the synapse (normally serotonin is allowed back in the axon terminal endings for release again). Blocking the reuptake allows serotonin to remain in the synaptic space longer and has the effect of supplying receiving neurons with more serotonin. However, Prozac affects all serotonin receptors in all parts of the brain at once—it is a shotgun effect. A risk exists for individuals who are not biochemically deprived in certain areas of the brain and who are then affected by an influx of biochemical activity that has an effect on other biochemicals and enzymes in the body (Cooper, Bloom & Roth, 1991). When dealing with normal students a more holistic and natural approach is to affect neurological and biochemical change through *experience* and *metaphorical imagination*; and these have much to do with a healthy classroom culture.

It is difficult to paint an accurate picture of the brain and its functions with the broad brush of a single neurotransmitter, like serotonin, because there are in fact no fewer than fourteen different serotonin receptors found in the brain. So, generalizing about the brain and behavior based on one aspect of a single neurotransmitter, without considering other factors, would be inappropriate and probably inaccurate. It is important to first determine where a biochemical is located in the brain before we can predict what its effect will be on the individual. No single gene and no single neurotransmitter can be held accountable for any given behavior, and no one neuron or neuronal circuit can be held accountable for personal action. It is a complex and holistic interplay between biochemicals, neurological connections, and electrical impulses that determines an individual's behavior and her or his interaction with the environment. The number and types of neuronal connections, the composition of biochemicals, and the polarity of electrical valences within the neurons are all important variables in determining what predisposes individuals to certain ideas, beliefs, and actions. Concomitantly, an individual's perception of the environment's reaction to her or his action affects all of these variables, and results in a new personalized construction of *reality*.

The brain's architecture and biochemistry mediate all individual perceptions of reality, and all individual realities are concealed in the genetic makeup of the individual's biochemistry and neuronal physiology. These individual realities, in turn, increase or decrease the likelihood that certain neuronal circuits or schemata will be activated and that certain action will be taken.

The Importance of Time

It takes *time* to construct the neuronal connections and transfer learning from short-term memory to long term memory. In his work with the marine snail, Aplysia, Eric Kandel (1992) found there is an important "consolidation" time after learning occurs that must be revered if the learning is to progress into long term memory. "Consolidation time" is a time when the proteins are phosphorylated and bind to genes with *cyclic AMP recognition element* in affected brain cells. If consolidation time is not allowed, the learning will not be transferred into long term memory and learning will fade from memory. So, *time* is critical to learning and memory and there is a need to provide time for consolidation after the learning is registered in the students' brains.

Time is also an important variable in the activation of neuronal circuits or schemata. In fact, time is such a critical variable to the activation of neuronal circuits that neuroscientists measure brain cell activity in *milliseconds*.

Phosphorylation can affect proteins that regulate the sodium and potassium channels in a brain cell. For example, protein kinases can alter sodium channels in the axon membrane of a brain cell. They act by "clogging up" some of the sodium gates so they cannot open during a nerve "firing" or impulse cascade. This form of protein kinase not only effects the brain cell's nerve impulse (the flow of electricity that precedes the discharge of neurotransmitters into the synaptic space), but it can also affect the brain cell's genetic coding. It can act indirectly upon genes and thus physically change the brain cell's function (Kandel, *et al.*, 1991; Levinthal, 1990; Ornstein & Thompson, 1984).

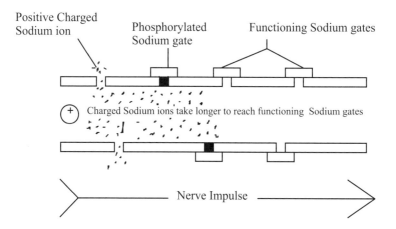

It is logical to think that the time it takes for a phosphorylated brain cell's nerve impulse to travel along the axon to the terminal endings is different than if the brain cell had not been affected by the process of phosphorylation. Likewise, obstructing the potassium channels has a similar effect by allowing "...calcium channels to be activated for longer periods, "which takes the brain cell more time to recover to a "resting state" enabling more neurotransmitters to be released into the synaptic space (Kandel & Hawkins, 1992, p. 83).

As mentioned earlier, a nerve impulse can travel between one kilometer per hour and two hundred kilometers per hour; and phosphorylation probably has some affect on the rate at which a nerve impulse "fires." Consider that the retarded electrical action of phosphorylated brain cells may be the tacit result of a perceived need in the individual to slow the activation of specific neuronal circuits or schemata. This slow response by phosphorylated brain cells allows for other brain cells with faster nerve impulses and recovery times to activate first.

The coherence of perception comes out of "time" rather than "space" itself (Damasio, 1994). There is no one place in the brain that holds meaning, rather meaning is acquired from many different parts of the brain through parallel processing of information and activation of schema. The faster brain cells are probably responsible for activating "stereotypical" neuronal circuits or schemata that are repeatedly used as responses to real and imagined stimuli. Certainly, there is little time wasted in activating these neuronal circuits as we almost subconsciously play out the stereotypical response. For students genetically predisposed to violence and whose environment is perceived as coercive and threatening, their stereotypical response to any problem situation or "sign stimulus" will probably be to activate some form of aggressive behavior. When these students feel little choice, their only recourse is to act out in a hostile fashion. Generally, it is a response that they have rehearsed and imagined many times and have fine tuned to achieve a desired response. However, if these students are given more *time* and opportunities to imagine different choices, these same students will probably learn to activate alternative neuronal circuits or schemata.

Neurological *time* and choice are important to us all, and when they are not accommodated problems can arise. *Time* and choice are great pacifiers. Two crucial components for maintaining a healthy "genetic" cycle of learning are *time* and context or choice. These two educational resources, that all professors have available to them, need to be used and judiciously administered in the teaching and learning relationship.

In theory, neuronal and biochemical adaptation, behavior, the reading of genes, experience within culture, and metaphorical imagination maintain a perfect "genetic" learning cycle. These elements contribute to the perpetual cognitive, affective, and psychomotor conditioning and reconditioning of every individual throughout her or his lifetime. However, in order to maintain a perfect "genetic" learning cycle, neurotransmitter activity has to be kept in balance through optimal biochemical synthesis and transmission, a phenomenon known as *homeostasis*. Too much or too little biochemical activity over a period of time can make us ill. Our physical/mental state can become unbalanced, offsetting the perfect nature of a healthy "genetic" learning cycle (Kandel, *et al.*, 1991; Levinthal, 1990; Restak, 1988; Beck & Beck, 1987, Ornstein & Thompson, 1984).

The Importance of Homeostasis

The brain/body strives for balance through moderation and optimization. Much of what the brain does is about inhibition, not excitement. If all the brain does is to excite the body, there would be no control at all. If there is too much activity, the brain/body becomes diseased and stressed. If there is too little activity, the brain/body becomes depressed and anxious. The brain/body constantly strives for a homeostatic balance. It wants to be healthy and normal. It is chiefly outside influences and individual perceptions of the environment that disturbs the homeostatic balance and affects the healthy genetic learning cycle of every individual.

Homeostasis and Endorphins

Endorphins (*Endo*genous Mor*phines*) are very powerful peptides, composed of small chains of amino acids. They act as neurotransmitters and are involved in maintaining health, mediating emotions, pain, and stress, and providing intrinsic reward (Kehoe, 1988). They perform these functions by relieving pain and/or inducing feelings of pleasure. There are three separate families of endorphins (Enkephalin, Beta-Endorphin, and Dynorphin) and there are many different endorphins within each family. Still, they all share an ability to induce feelings of euphoria and/or numb pain (Levinthal, 1988).

Endorphins are released from the terminal endings of neurons when animals are under stress and, in human beings, they may also be released in response to an emotional experience. Any stress or emotional experience, whether real or imagined, can sanction the release of multiple forms of endorphins. Hence, exposure to mediated experiences that provide new and exciting, stress inducing, and/or emotion laden sensory experience can stimulate the release of endorphins within the brain, resulting in a feeling of euphoria and/or "no pain." These mediated experiences may be in the form of viewing films, television programs, videotapes, plays, listening to the radio, CDs, tapes, pod-casts, reading books, magazines, newspapers, interacting with computer games, programs, and networks. Any or all of these media can affect various individuals, as long as the message is perceived as exciting, stressful, or emotion laden.

Avram Goldstein (1980) researched the effects of music and other stimuli that may stimulate endorphin release in individuals, which he said make it possible for subjects to experience a "thrill." A "thrill" he described as,

> ... a chill, shudder, tingling, or tickling. It may be accompanied by a feeling of "hair standing on end" or "goose bumps" on the arms. Thrills are invariably associated with sudden changes in mood or emotion. They may be accompanied by sighing, palpitation, tension of the jaw and facial muscles, a feeling of "lump in the throat," or incipient weeping. Some respondents noted a certain similarity of thrills to orgasm, but with many reservations concerning quality and intensity. Thrills were stated to be pleasurable... (p. 127)

Goldstein also observed,

> The typical stimulus that elicits a thrill is a confrontation with an emotionally stirring situation or event, such as a natural scene of transcendent beauty, a magnificent work of art or drama, a musical passage, a poignant personal encounter, a rousing speech, or a sudden intellectual insight. Even imagining these stimuli can be

effective. In people who experience thrills, there is invariably more than one kind of effective stimulus. The single generalization that seems to apply is that the thrills are associated with emotional arousal. (p. 127)

Goldstein concludes that it is "obvious conjecture" that these thrills are mediated by the endogenous opioids (endorphins) in our brain.

Endorphins have important biological roles to play in human survival. It is thought that endorphins help protect against pain by acting as a critical mechanism for avoiding pain. They are also involved with feelings of social comfort. In fact, some neuroscientists say endorphins may be responsible for feelings of positive reinforcement, which lead to repetitions of successful behavior (Levinthal, 1988). Endorphins are necessary and beneficial to the healthy human condition, provided they are distributed in a balanced and optimum fashion (Beck & Beck, 1987). In other words, their homeostatic balance is of great importance to the healthy operation of every individual.

Endorphins can be physically addicting in exactly the same way heroin and morphine can be physically addicting (Kandel, *et al.*, 1991; Gathercoal, 1990; Levinthal, 1988; Kehoe, 1988; Beck & Beck, 1987; Ornstein & Thompson, 1984). In fact, all humans are addicted to endorphins. We physically need them. We must maintain an optimum amount of endorphin activity in the brain in order to remain "normal," just as a heroin addict needs an optimum "fix" injected into her or his blood stream to remain "normal." Endorphins are different, however, in that they do not have to be injected; they are already in our bodies and simply need to be normally synthesized and released. We remain healthy and normal when our endorphin activity is complementary to our physical needs.

Think of healthy endorphin activity as a bell shaped curve. Our health (on one continuum) is "perfect" when the optimum amount of endorphin activity is present (on the other continuum). This is the healthy homeostatic balance the brain/body strives to maintain.

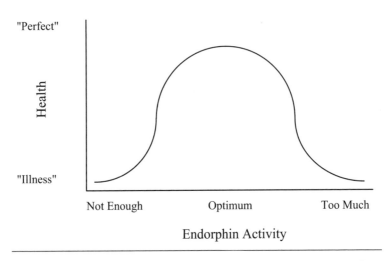

"Perfect"

Health

"Illness"

Not Enough   Optimum   Too Much

Endorphin Activity

Our health is affected when there is an *oversupply* of endorphin activity, which may be signaled starting with a "high" or a "thrill." It is also affected when there is an *under supply* of endorphin activity, which leads to symptoms of opiate withdrawal and a very strong desire for more endorphin activity.

To illustrate this point, a parallel can be drawn between an endorphin under supply and the symptoms of heroin addiction withdrawal. Heroin addicts display withdrawal symptoms of panic, distress, a display of sorrowful emotion, and a strong desire to be reunited with their source of immediate gratification. Similarly, as endorphin levels become low, people may seek out the social stimulation that will reduce their distress and produce a form of reward or reinforcement for their social interaction. The source of their social interaction can be imagined or real, mediated or a real-life encounter.

An individual's reliance on endorphin activity in the brain becomes unhealthy as it nears a stage of "addiction." At that time, the homeostatic balance of endorphin activation fluctuates greatly between the individual's physical need and the amount of endorphin activity. Endorphin "addictions" can be discussed in many forms, e.g., workaholics, sexaholics, exerciseaholics, or mediaholics. This appendix will address the role of the electronic media as a distracter to teaching and learning and inhibitor of pro-social behaviors, although the reader can substitute other social addictions into this discussion.

Television and other electronic media can induce endorphin activity in an individual's brain and they are in direct competition with book study, classroom teaching and learning, and the development of intellectual insights resulting from reading and classroom teaching as sources for endorphin synthesis and release. In illustration, studies conducted by pediatricians have consistently found a perfect negative correlation between the number of hours students watch television and their scores on standardized tests. The more students watch television, the worse their test scores and vice-versa.

Many of today's students may find feelings of reward and relief by viewing and listening to the messages of the media rather than activating endorphins through "real-world" interactions. It may be that some students are *addicted* to the "reel-world" of electronic media as a source for maintaining an optimum level of endorphin activity in the brain and stimulating the occasional "thrill," all of which can lead to repetitive behavior. "When endorphin levels are low,... there is an innate tendency to seek social stimulation. These social stimuli then lead to a release of endorphins that not only reduces the separation distress but also produces reinforcement or reward for the behaviors of social interaction" (Levinthal, 1988, p. 145).

Some students spend so much time viewing television that they perceive the television personalities as their "friends." By spending social time with them, vicariously through the stories on television, students experience endorphin release in the brain. Some may empathize with the characters as they share in the loves, friendships, and sorrows of their favorites. When we are addicted our view of the future is narrowed and almost nothing but the here and now is processed with clarity. Isn't it fascinating that most people care more about which news personality is anchoring the television news report than the news reports and world affairs presented on the newscast.

This idea of *addiction to media messages* fits well with

DeFleur and Ball-Rokeach's (1990) dependency theory. Dependency theory suggests that individuals are actively involved in constructing their own personal media system; and these systems provide individuals with personal rewards to the extent that individuals become dependent upon the media system he or she creates. Endorphin activity in the brain may be the source of reward associated with a personally constructed media system. These addicting neurotransmitters may ultimately be responsible for creating an individual need and/or desire for daily exposure to certain media messages and mediated experiences. Think about it—what media messages are you exposed to daily without which you would not feel "normal?" Do you need your daily newspaper or a dose of sports programming on television? Can you go without browsing the World-Wide Web or accessing your email? Is there a favorite computer game that demands your constant attention?

Endorphins are a necessary "drug." People strive to feel "normal" by maintaining an optimum level of endorphin activity (Levinthal, 1988). For individuals who are addicted to mediated experience as a source for stimulating endorphin activity, feeling normal may mean spending 20-30 hours per week with certain media messages; and for others, it may mean spending up to 90 hours per week. We all have different biological needs. For those who need heavy exposure to media messages there can be adverse effects on their health.

One health effect is *desensitization*. If media messages are stressful and/or thrilling they can induce endorphin activity and endorphins act on our brain cells like drugs (Gathercoal, 1990).

> When the brain is flooded with an unusually large quantity of a drug, the nerve cells respond by cutting down the number of receptors. That's why drug abusers need more and more of the drug to get the same effect. Then, when the drug is taken away, the brain's *natural* chemicals have fewer receptors to lock onto . . . the result is an increase in anxiety and "nervous excitement." That's withdrawal . . . . Opiates such as morphine and heroin produce an intense withdrawal reaction (Restak, 1988, p. 132-133).

Endorphins connect to the same receptors as heroin and morphine. Have you ever had a friend come over for dinner, only to have them leave early so they could get home in time to watch a favorite television program? Have you ever tried to call the children to the dinner table as they sit "deaf" in front of the television or when they are playing a computer game? Could it be that these children are in a mediated "opium" induced state of numbness and pleasure?

Media messages allow individuals opportunities for vicarious rehearsal of life experience, and as a result individuals are conditioning their brain/bodies to be incapable of fully appreciating a similar "real-world" experience in their own lives. By previewing stressful and/or emotional portrayals of life experiences on television and other electronic media, people are neurologically and biochemically adapting to handle similar stress and pain in their "real-world" lives. So the next time these individuals see someone killed in cold blood, whether real or mediated, it is not likely to be so shocking; and the individual may respond with, "I've seen worse."

Research conducted by Yoshio Hosobuchi at the University of California in San Francisco in 1977 supports this notion of building a tolerance to endorphin activity. Hosobuchi attached electrodes to the PAG (periaqueductal gray) region of the brain in six patients suffering chronic pain from cancer. A hand-held, battery-operated transmitter was used to stimulate endorphin activity in the PAG region. As a result, five of the six patients no longer had to take opiate drugs and they reported total relief from pain. However, the hand-held transmitter had to be used sparingly, in short bursts and with a period of rest in between, otherwise the patients would build up a tolerance and the stimulation would be ineffective (Levinthal, 1988). This supports the notion that too much endorphin activity can lead to desensitization and habituation that is marked by the retraction of synaptic connections in the PAG region of the brain.

In essence, individuals can move their homeostatic need for endorphins further along the "normal" continuum. The resulting physical condition is one where more and more endorphin activity is needed in order to feel "normal" (Kandel, *et al.*, 1991; Levinthal, 1990; Ornstein & Thompson, 1984).

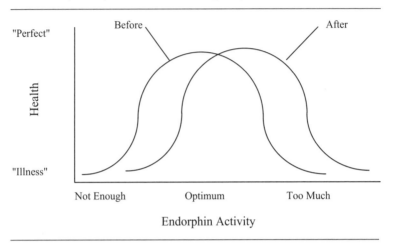

As the chart indicates, the affected individual will need even more endorphin activity, more often, in the future in order to feel "normal" the next time she or he encounters a similar stress inducing and/or emotion laden experience.

Another health effect related to endorphin activity is closely linked to modeling theory. DeFleur and Ball-Rokeach (1990) explain,

> The media are a readily available and attractive source of models. They provide symbolic modeling of almost every conceivable form of behavior. A rich literature has shown that both children and adults acquire attitudes, emotional responses, and new styles of conduct from all the media, and especially from films and television. (p. 216)

There may be a carry-over effect from media messages to real life. Consider that media messages can affect strong endorphin "thrills" and that the accompanying metaphorical imaginations associated with this endorphin activity is very memorable to the individual (Goldstein, 1980). Such positive feelings, associated with endorphin activating media messages, may motivate students to experiment with their imaginings in the "real world" environment. A girl or boy may transfer her or his imagined behavior to "real world" action in response to problematic situations and in hopes of achieving positive reinforcement in the form of a similar or even greater "thrill" than was ever imagined while viewing and listening to the media message.

Endorphins and Morality

Most film and television media messages preach at the audience. They do not often allow the audience the opportunity to work through moral dilemmas associated with the stories they tell. Instead, they usually provide the context/problem, and the solution. In this regard they act as moral dictators operating at the lowest levels of moral development. The implicit principles on which many of the moral decisions are based are rarely made explicit. Instead, the audience is shown behavior and not cognition or feelings.

...young children are often unable to relate a series of complex actions to their final consequence. Thus, when industry spokespersons claim that their programs are fundamentally prosocial because good ultimately triumphs over bad, they ignore this important finding. The young child is much less likely to make the interpretive connection and, therefore, less likely to learn the moral lesson. (Rubinstein, 1983, p. 821-822)

Television simplifies moral dilemmas and models lower level moral problem-solving for complex problems. Often the stories television tells are glorified by peer group interaction. Students talk about things that happened, concentrating on endorphin activating happenings within the message, ignoring critical aspects of the story that are not new, novel, exciting or culturally significant as "sign stimulus."

Television has a direct visual link to the limbic system (the emotional center of the brain) via a neuronal network originally designed to detect changes in odor through the sense of smell. A significant feature of this sensory center is that it was designed to block out different odors after a period of time and think of the environment as normal. The system would only activate again when the odor changes. Now, the area has evolved to include visual information as well. This is why the brain responds to new or novel visual information and disregards things that appear to be "normal." It is a legacy of our pre-historic past (Levinthal, 1988).

So, students who view many hours of high action/high violence films and television often find real life "dull and boring." When attempting to transfer modeled behaviors from the film and television world to the "real world," students may not experience the euphoric reward they experienced while watching actors perform the same actions on the screen. This can be frustrating for the individual. When they try to emulate the imagined experience, they may have lost the ability to fully appreciate the real experience because they have been desensitized. If an oversupply of endorphin activity is present in an individual it would not be natural for them to find intrinsic rewards in the same way a "normal" individual would find reward through social relationships. Such individuals might be unable to display appropriate emotional responses in social settings; they may have no biochemical need to interact with others. As well, they may not fully appreciate the consequences of inflicting physical pain on others and would display a general lack of emotion (Levinthal, 1988). Given these arguments regarding endorphin activation and desensitization and modeling via certain media messages, it can be argued that exposing children to television programs, computer games, and other powerful media messages, without providing them with a context for understanding, is a form of child abuse; a form of social deprivation.

Endorphins and Anxiety

Media messages that make students feel anxious can also stimulate endorphin activity. When students expose themselves to media messages that generate feelings of anxiety (horror and suspense films can do this) their bodies release neurotransmitters that attach themselves to "anxiety" receptors. This action makes them feel nervous and distraught. Since the human body has no tranquility receptors to bring them down from these feelings of anxiety, endorphins are released to provide analgesia and a feeling of euphoria that simulates and encourages tranquil behaviors (Kandel, *et al.*, 1991). Media messages that make students anxious, such as horror and suspense films, arcade type computer games with life and death scenarios, and emotion laden news, promote the release of endorphins in response to feelings of anxiety. In this way, endorphins are also implicated and play an important role in *desensitization* to horrific mediated and real life events. At the same time, they help to create a physical dependency that encourages individuals to seek out some similar experiences, which provide them with feelings of anxiety and concomitant feelings of "tranquility." This may explain why so many people "enjoy" films and video that portray violent acts and that are classified for Restricted Audiences Only (S.A. Council for children's Films and Television, Inc., 1986). Many of today's children like to scare themselves, because it feels good when the endorphins are activated.

Many of our students probably find high action/high violence media messages irresistibly stressful, causing the release of copious amounts of endorphins and inducing a trance-like state interrupted only by the occasional "thrill" which then sedates them again by dulling their pain. It's hard for real life experiences to match that level of endogenous reward. After children, in particular, have grown used to the thrills and chills of high action/high violence media messages, their classroom activities, family picnics, and other sources of real-live-action social situations may seem ordinary and unsatisfactory. As a result, they may display an inability to respond emotionally to social relationships and affection, or appreciate the full impact of pain; they may also display a lack of desire for companionship, and a persistence with repetitive patterns (stereotypical responses) that are not associated with external reinforcement (Levinthal, 1988).

Some neuroscientists believe "Socially appropriate behavior may be learned through the reduction of anxiety that comes when one decides *not* to engage in antisocial behavior" (Restak,

1988, p. 312). These individuals find feelings of anxiety uncomfortable and avoid them by creating an environmental context where neurons that release neurotransmitters that attach themselves to "anxiety" receptors are inhibited. However, there are other individuals who may find that anxiety is pleasurable, due to the accompanying release of endorphins; and these individuals may escalate their antisocial behavior in search of the endorphin release that flows along with feelings of anxiety. Consider that many of today's students who are predisposed to violence and who enjoy more and more endorphin activity may become caught up in their own pleasure and be desensitized to the needs and interests of their living environment. Such a mentality can result from increased anxiety emanating from exposure to high action/high violence media messages. These students' perceptions of their immediate environment will be dramatically different from "normal" students' perceptions. Consider the following news accounts as artifacts of our modern world and speculate about connections between violent mediated experience and real-life behavior. Could there be an anxiety/endorphin connection?

Queen Street killer's diary...

Diaries kept by the Queen Street killer, Frank Vitkovic, 22, showed developing insanity and admiration for the bullet-spraying movie cult hero Rambo, police say.

And at a police Press conference yesterday, further details of the former Melbourne University student's private life were released, including the fact that about 10 of 27 videos found in his bedroom were murder movies, many of them taped directly from television.

On Vitkovic's bedroom wall hung a huge color poster of Rambo in action, and a clipping about the fictitious warmonger, played by actor Sylvester Stallone, was found among his possessions. (*The Advertiser*, Saturday, December 12, 1987, p. 3)

Bundy: "I deserve...punishment"

Condemned killer Ted Bundy told an interviewer ...

that he "felt the full range of guilt and remorse" but that he had it "compartmentalized" in his brain.

He said it was "important to me that I'm not blaming pornography ... I take full responsibility." But he said hard-core pornography "guided and shaped" what he did.

After he committed his first murder, "What were the emotional effects on you? What happened in the days after that?" Dobson asked.

"It was like coming out of some horrible trance. ... It was like being possessed by something so awful, so alien."

"I was absolutely horrified that I was capable of doing something like that." (*Corvallis Gazette-Times*, Wednesday, January 25, 1989, p. A3)

Damasio (1994) found subjects with frontal lobe brain damage who were shown highly emotive pictures of homicides did not behave normally, and physiologically they were abnormal. These abnormal patients were able to describe, in words, "the fear, disgust, or sadness of the pictures they saw," but they did not exhibit the typical body-state associated with the viewing of horrific photographs (p. 210). The patients' somatic-markers or "gut feelings" in response to seeing the pictures were not present. Extending on from Damasio's finding, could it be that when an individual's emotional system is overloaded with neurological and biochemical activity, when the homeostatic need for biochemical activity is significantly shifted, an individual's thought processes are clouded and the normal somatic marker responses are neutralized by the high endorphin activity associated with "thrills" and emotional exuberance?

Boy, 5, stabs toddler...

A five-year-old boy made a bizarre stabbing frenzy assault on a toddler playmate—apparently "inspired" by two horror movies.

He lunged and stabbed the 2-1/2-year-old girl 17 times, wounding her in the thighs, buttocks and face.

A witness told police that before the bloody rampage

in Boston the boy was talking about "Jason," the ice-hockey-masked killer in the horror film *Friday the 13th* and *"Freddy Krueger,"* the grotesque character who killed children with razor-like claws in *A Nightmare On Elm Street.*

The boy apparently had seen both of the violent films on television. (*The Advertiser*, Saturday, November 21, 1987, p. 6)

Consider, also, this account from James Vance, who after a prolonged bout of drinking and listening to songs by the heavy metal group *"Judas Priest"* made a death pact with his friend Ray. His friend, Ray, put a shotgun to his throat and pulled the trigger. James Vance shot himself, but flinched at the critical moment and survived, although facially disfigured. He remembers the night he shot himself:

And [Ray] said, "I sure fucked my life up." There was blood everywhere. I picked up the shotgun. I had no doubt in my mind, no second thoughts. I knew I was gonna' shoot myself. I was afraid; I didn't want to die... But I have—I mean, I was going to shoot myself. It was like I had no control over it. Cause I didn't want to die... And... I shot myself. (From *Dream Deceivers*, Produced and Directed by David Van Taylor, 1991)

Later, James had this to say about the effect the music by the heavy metal group *"Judas Priest"* had on him and his friend Ray:

Judas Priest sang a lot about the cosmos... Songs like "Epitaph," "Dreamer," and "Dream Deceiver" the music was just beautiful. We would get power from it and our emotions would just soar with the music... and then they would go up and down and up and down... *It was like a drug, like a narcotic and it wasn't just this one night [when Ray took his life and James shot himself]. It was always like that.* (From *Dream Deceivers*, Produced and Directed by David Van Taylor, 1991)

How much "free will" do we really have over our actions? In human beings, the frontal lobes of the brain have developed more than any other creature on Earth; enabling people to predict the consequences of their actions and operate within the social expectations of the group. This is commonly referred to as "free will." However, new developments in neuroscience indicate that:

> ...a body-based mechanism is needed to assist "cool" reason; it is also true that some of those body-based signals can impair the quality of reasoning... I see some failures of rationality as not just due to a primary calculation weakness, but also due to the influence of biological drives such as obedience, conformity, the desire to preserve self-esteem, which are often [made] manifest as emotions and feelings. (Damasio, 1994, p. 191)

How much "free will" is exercised when students strive to meet the social expectations attached to our rights and responsibilities of citizenship?

The Importance of Context and a Healthy Classroom Culture

Context is very important when talking about addiction. In her book, *Mindfulness*, Ellen J. Langer (1989) talks about addiction and context. She reports "...that heroin addicts are less likely to report withdrawal if they don't consider themselves addicts. Those who take the same amount of heroin and call themselves addicts often suffer much greater withdrawal symptoms" (p. 183). Those who do not see themselves as addicts may use alternative neurological pathways that are not dependent upon the drug.

Langer (1989) cites the experience of Vietnam veterans as an example of alternative contexts affecting addiction. She points out that as the United States withdrew troops from the overseas conflict Veterans' Administration (VA) hospitals were warned of the large numbers of soldiers who would need rehabilitation from heroin addiction. Yet, when the troops returned home, few showed up at the VA hospitals for treatment. So, when no one was showing up for rehabilitation, the VA went out and asked the soldiers what was going on? The soldiers then readily admitted that when they were in Vietnam they needed and used heroin, but when they returned home, they just didn't need it anymore. "Our perceptions and interpretations influence the way our bodies respond. *When the 'mind' is in a context, the 'body' is necessarily also in that context.* To achieve a different physiological state, sometimes what we need to do is to place the mind in another context" (Langer, 1989, p. 177). It appears that there are several ways of accomplishing this task of placing the mind/body in a different context. One way is to move to a new environment, another is prayer or meditation, and others involve the use of drug therapy. These contextual change agents have real implications for culture and the teaching and learning relationship.

When a problem situation develops and we find ourselves in the throes of emotion filled activity, professors and students need to learn to take time. Time and contemplation of choices keep us from acting too quickly or relying on "stereotypical response" mechanisms. It's more than the old adage, "Count to ten before you act." Individuals need to bring their mind/body state to a conscious level. We need to learn to recognize when emotions are high and the euphoria of the moment is in charge. We need to learn to control our emotions by taking time to think; withholding actions until the action can be evaluated via a balanced state of biochemistry that mediates holistically the individual's cognitive, emotional, and behavioral predispositions.

Providing students with the knowledge of how our addictions can affect our brain architecture and biochemistry, and concomitantly our thinking and action, is one step towards generating a new context for thinking about possible behaviors. For example, when one of the author's son was in High School, he invited a friend over to play video games. As the two were beginning to play the games, the author touched his son on the shoulder and asked him, "Can you handle this?" The son assured him that he could. The author reminded him of other times he had played at length and how his actions, after play, were aggressive and spontaneous. They talked of the endorphin "thrill" and the biochemical imbalance that was about to take place and the son again assured the author that he could handle the situation. As it happened, he did handle the situation well and played for some hours with his friend. The knowledge of this neuro-biochemical phenomenon did much to help him control his anxiety during and after play and to take the time needed to deal rationally with problem situations. As a result of his deliberation and thoughtfulness, he was able to create a different context for living and learning. He was able to take time and deliberately think of himself in another context, and thereby bypass the neurological pathways associated with endorphin "thrills" and video games play.

When professors practice teaching and learning strategies complementary with *The Judicious Professor*, it helps students to construct a context that is perceived as fair, free, and caring. When a student truly believes that this is the state of the environment, the students are more likely to think of themselves as having value and as a result, they will be less likely to act out against people and things in the environment.

Will using strategies complementary with *The Judicious Professor* solve all our problems in education? The answer is "no." In fact, there will continue to be problems. However, *using these teaching and learning strategies will not make things worse*, and *they have the potential to make things better*. Professors who establish mutual goals and expectations through mutual respect are less likely to be victims of revenge. Consider that some, not many, but some students display thinking and behavior like this:

> ...signs of irrational thinking are usually absent. They are egocentric and lack the capacity to feel empathy and love. They have little or no conscience or sense of guilt; tend to project blame when they get into trouble. They are unreliable, untruthful, and insincere, but they are often convincing because they believe their own lies. There is a vast gulf between what they say and what they do. They are impulsive, the whim of the moment being paramount. They are given to periodic and often senseless antisocial behavior which may be either aggressive or passive and parasitic. (Restak, 1988, p. 310)

This is the description of the violent psychopath. For these people, few relationship strategies will work well. They are abnormal. However, the professor who employs strategies complementary with *The Judicious Professor* always avoids power struggles and encourages students to take calculated risks and to be responsible for their actions. In this way, the professor remains on the same side as the student and is never viewed as the problem. The professor remains learner-centered, maintaining a role of mentor and guide when the student is in times of trouble. The professor remains the educator, armed with resources for teaching and learning and embracing student behavior problems as simply another opportunity to teach.

Professors need to establish and maintain a healthy classroom culture. A healthy classroom culture helps students to contextualize violent and emotion-laden media messages by offering a framework for discussing the dichotomy of modal values that exists between most commercial media messages and the modal values advocated by institutions of higher education. This is best achieved when professors take a learner-centered approach to teaching and learning; an approach that gives students a sense of "permanent value" (Dreikurs, 1968).

For example, if the "rules of civility" are broken, the professor needs to take the time to listen to students. Then, the professor must act with professional courage, working in the student's best interests to restore relationships and property that may have been damaged by a breach in rules. With this thoughtful, professional approach, the professor is sending a powerful message about the importance of the individual student, all the while mentoring him or her in ways to restore and recover from a problem situation. This kind of teaching and learning relationship is antithetical to the behavior generally displayed in commercial films and television. When modeling such alternative behavior for students, the judicious professor is laying a context, a fabric of neurological connections, which helps prepare their students for ideological change and responsible citizenship in a free, democratic society. This is the antithesis to coercive, stimulus/response models portrayed on most television shows and in films. For many professors and students, it is completely different from current discipline practices in institutions of higher education, the home, or even discussed in the media. It provides professors with opportunities to challenge students' neuronal circuits by offering students "neurological time" and options to consider. It allows us all to transcend the lower levels of moral development and operate at a principled level. Imagine the opportunities for teaching and learning when a student with a problem is met by a professor, who intuitively says, "Tell me about it."

Appendix II

Are You Perceived as a Judicious Professor?

When professors and students begin courses by establishing mutual expectations and goals they do much to weave a cultural fabric where students take responsibility for learning and the professor is perceived as a wise, loyal, educational leader. We have found that when *The Judicious Professor* is employed as a foundation for building relationships, professors favorably contribute to students' social development, urging them toward autonomy, and they better prepare students for living and learning in a democratic society.

Professors may ask, "How do we know when we are successfully building this culture of responsibility in our college and university courses?" One instrument that can be used to reflect on the effect *The Judicious Professor* is having on students in courses is a questionnaire developed by The Social Development Group, Research Branch of the South Australian Department of Education, and published in their 1980 book, *Developing the Classroom Group*. This questionnaire has been used repeatedly in college and university courses to ascertain students' levels of social development and provide professors and students with one measure that sheds light on the "health and culture" of relationships with and between students.

Appendix II

Social Development Questionnaire

Directions: For each statement mark whether it is true or false for this class with this professor.

	True	False
1. This professor nearly always tells us what to do.	❏	❏
2. We have to do what the professor says in this class.	❏	❏
3. The whole class helped to make the class rules.	❏	❏
4. I often decide for myself what I will do and where I will do it in this class.	❏	❏
5. We are all very friendly together in this class.	❏	❏
6. When students argue in this class people get upset.	❏	❏
7. Nearly all of this class feels warm and friendly toward this professor.	❏	❏
8. It's okay to disagree strongly with this professor.	❏	❏

Download the Social Development Questionnaire at this URL: http://www.dock.net/gathercoal/socialdevelopment

---

The social development questionnaire differentiates between power and affect relationships through a series of eight true/false questions and places a student's response in one of four developmental groups "dependent," "rebellion," "cohesion," and "autonomy." Students' levels of social development are quantified to measure four attributes of the classroom culture—two attributes dealing with power: "professor power" and "student power," and two relationship attributes: "student/student relationships" and "professor/student relationships." The "professor power" attribute represents how much power the professor holds in the classroom versus the student's sense of power. The "student power" attribute represents how much individual power students feel they have versus other students in the classroom. The "student/ student relationships" attribute represents how well all students get along with each other in the class; and the "professor/student relationships" attribute represents how well all students get along with their professor.

Descriptions of each stage of social development follow:

In *stage 1*, the main issue is dependence. Students are generally dependent and submissive, and do what the [professor] says. The students' interaction is mostly through the [professor], so there is low covert interaction among students. There is little disruptive behavior, but some "attention getting." Order is fairly high. Anxiety levels are high in some students. Some students are bored. Motivation is extrinsic; approval, praise and encouragement from [professor] and [significant others] is important. There is fear of punishment.

In *stage 2* the main issue is rebellion. The students test, challenge, and try out the [professor]. The student group separates into two camps, one in opposition to the [professor], the other seeking to maintain dependent group behavior. Some students challenge or ignore the [professor]'s efforts to control the class. Noise level tends to be high. Trust level among students is low, and aggressive interactions and put downs are common. The rebellious sub-group is extrinsically motivated by peer group approval, moderated by fear of [professor] punishment. The intrinsic motivation is for autonomy, moderated by dependency needs.

In *stage 3*, the main issue is cohesion. Students are friendly and trusting to each other and the [professor]. There is very little disruptive behavior. There is a lot of interaction but of an orderly type. They conform to group norms. There is little disagreement, as this is seen as disruptive to the harmony of the group. This inability to handle conflict results in some covert bad feeling. Extrinsic motivation comes from praise and encouragement from peer group and [professor]. Breach of class norms brings strong group disapproval.

Autonomy is the main issue at *stage 4*. Individuals are self-directed, able to seek and give support, but function well without it. Students take responsibility for their own learning. There is a high level of interaction. Agreement and discussion are the norm; agreement occurs in the context of disagreement.

Feelings (positive and negative) are openly expressed. Students work the same with or without the [professor] present. Disruptive behavior is virtually non-existent. Students show flexibility and adaptability in a variety of learning situations without demanding conformity of all members. They utilize self-awareness and empathy rather than rules to choose behavior. Motivation is mainly intrinsic. Social behavior is based on respect for self and others. Learning is seen as a way of gaining personal competence and joy. (Education Department of South Australia, 1980, pp. 31 - 35)

Note that the description for Autonomy, or the 4th stage of social development, closely parallels Kohlberg's (1976) fifth stage of moral development (the principled stage or "social contract theory" stage).

Since the questionnaire measures four attributes, it is possible that one student can respond at the "dependent" stage for "professor power," the "rebellion" stage for "student power," the "cohesive" stage for "student/student relationships," and the "autonomous" stage for "professor/student relationships." When scoring the above example, the questionnaire indicates one count for each stage of social development for that student. In other words, students will tally four scores for each completed questionnaire. (See directions for scoring the questionnaire at the end of this appendix—online resource is available, too). By collecting this information for every student in the class, the professor is able to measure central tendencies and reflect on ways to improve the "health and culture" of the course.

For years, we have used this social development questionnaire as a pre-test/post-test in college and university courses and workshops. Our results have been consistent and positive, albeit never perfect. In every case, we have been able to move students from the lower dependent stages of social development to stages of autonomy within a few hours of beginning class. Following are examples of two of our questionnaire results:

Students: Preservice teachers in full-time, fifth-year teacher education program.
Course: EDTP520 Leadership, Management and Law in Diverse Classrooms.
When: Fall Semester 2000; Tuesdays from 1-4 p.m. weekly for fifteen weeks.

Pre-Test: August 2000. Number of responses and percentage of responses for each level of social development:

Dependent	Rebellion	Cohesion	Autonomy
N=9 11%	N=5 6%	N=16 19%	N=54 64%

Pre-Test: Average student response rating for the four attributes of social development: professor power, student power, student/student relationships and professor/student relationship.

Average Student Response Rating			
Power Relationships		AffectRelationships	
Professor Power	Student Power	Student/ Student	Professor/ Student
2.6	3.1	3.8	3.9

It is important that the pre-test is the first activity conducted when beginning a new course. Students need to complete the pre-test prior to viewing the syllabus or before addressing the curriculum. As soon as students enter the room, hand them a questionnaire and encourage them to make a choice between "true" or "false" for each of the eight statements. Instruct them that if they don't know the answer to a question, they should guess, but they need to make a definitive decision of "true" or "false" for each statement.

When viewing the pre-test data, above, it is evident that these students come to class with a high level of autonomy and cohesion. They have been in a cohort group for at least one semester and this kind of social development is reasonable to expect from this group. Viewing the average student response rating provides greater insight into the class "health and culture." While the affect relationships are very high, the power relationships are comparatively suffering. This is where *The*

Judicious Professor can help improve the "health and culture" of the class.

The second activity conducted in the course is to establish expectations for the professor, the students, and the course of instruction. Then, compare the course syllabus with the expectations of the course of instruction to determine whether the professor and students are pursuing the same goals. Establishing mutual expectations and goals is critical to the implementation of *The Judicious Professor*. Remember, this philosophy is "front loading" and establishing a social contract for relationships and academic expectations does much to lay a foundation for further dialog.

Five weeks later, after twelve hours of instructional time, the questionnaire was administered as a post-test.

Post-Test: October 2000. Number of responses and percentage of responses for each level of social development.

Dependent	Rebellion	Cohesion	Autonomy
N=2 2%	N=3 3%	N=8 9%	N=75 85%

Post-Test: Average student response rating for the four attributes of social development: professor power, student power, student/student relationships, and professor/student relationship.

Average Student Response Rating			
Power Relationships		Affect Relationships	
Professor Power	Student Power	Student/ Student	Professor/ Student
3.7	3.9	3.5	4.0

Note the increase in autonomy. It is now 85% of the total responses and note that dependent and rebellious responses are almost non-existent. The average student response ratings, too, tell a story of student empowerment. This pre-test/post-test result has been mirrored many times. Since 1995, we often use this questionnaire when teaching a course or conducting a workshop. We have never had a negative return on this questionnaire, we always end up moving students toward autonomy, and the cultural transformation has been almost immediate. We have found that the classroom culture can shift very rapidly. Below are pretest and posttest results for a one-day, seven-hour workshop we conducted in 2003.

Pre-Test: August 25, 2003, 8:45 a.m. Number of responses and percentage of responses for each level of social development.

Dependent	Rebellion	Cohesion	Autonomy
N=91 32%	N=37 13%	N=99 35%	N=57 20%

Pre-Test: Average student response rating for the four attributes of social development: professor power, student power, student/student relationships and professor/student relationship.

Average Student Response Rating			
Power Relationships		Affect Relationships	
Professor Power	Student Power	Student/ Student	Professor/ Student
1.7	2.4	2.9	2.7

Post-Test: August 25, 2003, 2:30 p.m. Number of responses and percentage of responses for each level of social development.

Dependent	Rebellion	Cohesion	Autonomy
N=23 9%	N=16 6%	N=66 25%	N=159 60%

Post-Test: Average student response rating for the four attributes of social development: professor power, student power, student/student relationships and professor/student relationship.

Average Student Response Rating			
Power Relationships		Affect Relationships	
Professor Power	Student Power	Student/ Student	Professor/ Student
3.0	3.5	3.3	3.7

Scoring the Questionnaire

1. There are 8 statements that are scored in four pairs. Each pair of statements give four possible results, e.g., the first pair is questions 1

and 2, and they deal with the attribute of Professor Power in the classroom.

		True	False
If a student marked as follows:	Statement 1.	☒	❑
	Statement 2.	☒	❑

this would be a stage 1 or S.1. response (see rubric below).

The three other possible responses follow:

	True	False
Statement 1.	☒	❑
Statement 2.	❑	☒

a S.2. response

	True	False
Statement 1.	❑	☒
Statement 2.	☒	❑

a S.3. response

	True	False
Statement 1.	❑	☒
Statement 2.	❑	☒

a S.4. response

We can summarize these four responses as follows.

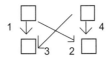

If you read the statements and look at the scoring system you will see how they fit into the stages of social development model.

The overall scoring scheme is this:

1.
2.
3.
4.

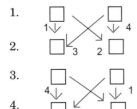

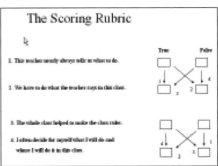

The Scoring Rubric

5.
6.
7.
8.

Analysis of the Questionnaire

The first four statements deal with power and the last four statements deal with affect.

On each questionnaire write the stage numbers beside each pair of questions, e.g.

Directions: For each statement mark whether it is true or false for this class with this professor.

	True	False	Score
1. This professor nearly always tells us what to do.	☒	☐	1
2. We have to do what the professor says in this class.	☒	☐	
3. The whole class helped to make the class rules.	☒	☐	3
4. I often decide for myself what I will do and where I will do it in this class.	☐	☒	
5. We are all very friendly together in this class.	☐	☒	1
6. When students argue in this class people get upset.	☒	☐	
7. Nearly all this class feels warm and friendly toward this professor.	☐	☒	1
8. It's okay to disagree strongly with this professor.	☐	☒	

Total the scores from the class under the four stages, e.g., using the data from the above example:

S.1. Dependency	S.2. Rebellion	S.3. Cohesion	S.4. Autonomy
3	0	1	0

The class result may look something like this:

S.1. Dependency	S.2. Rebellion	S.3. Cohesion	S.4. Autonomy
27	14	9	10

This can be converted to a percentage by adding up the total number of responses, e.g.,

$$27 + 14 + 9 + 10 = 60$$

and dividing the stage totals by this number, e.g.,

$$\frac{27}{60} \qquad \frac{14}{60} \qquad \frac{9}{60} \qquad \frac{10}{60}$$

and multiplying by $\frac{100}{1}$ to get a percentage, e.g.

S.1. Dependency	S.2. Rebellion	S.3. Cohesion	S.4. Autonomy
45%	23%	15%	17%

We have developed an Excel spreadsheet that will automatically compute the total numbers and percentages and the average student response rating for each of the four social development attributes, professor power, student power, student/student relationships and professor/student relationships. This spreadsheet is available for download at this URL:

http://www.dock.net/gathercoal/socialdevelopment

With this spreadsheet downloaded to your computer, all you need to do is enter the score for each pair of questions and the spreadsheet will automatically provide you with the results of your questionnaire. See example on the next page.

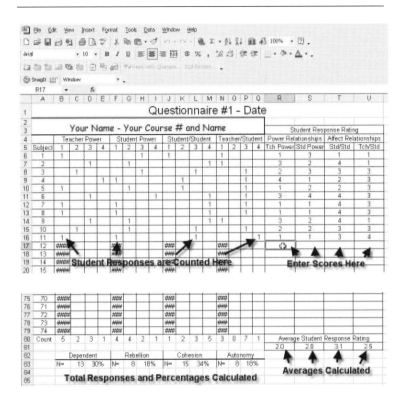

References

Advertiser Newspaper. (Nov. 21, 1987). Boy, 5, stabs toddler: Horror films blamed, p. 6, published Adelaide, South Australia.

Advertiser Newspaper. (Dec. 12, 1987). Queen street killer's diary showed "developing insanity", p. 3, published Adelaide, South Australia.

Bachevalier, J. (1990). Ontogenetic development of habit and memory formation in primates. In A. Diamond (Ed.), *The development and neural bases of higher cognitive functions.* New York: The New York Academy of Sciences.

Beck, D., & Beck, J. (1987). *The pleasure connection.* San Francisco: Synthesis Press.

Cooper, J., Boom, F., & Roth, R. (1991). *The biochemical basis of neuropharmacology*, 6th Ed. New York: Oxford University Press.

Corvallis Gazette-Times Newspaper. (Jan. 25, 1989). Bundy: "I deserve...punishment," p. A3, published Corvallis, OR.

Damasio, A. (1994). *Descartes' error: Emotion, reason, and the human brain.* New York: G.P. Putnam's Sons.

DeFleur, M., & Ball-Rokeach, S. (1990). *Theories of mass communication*, 5th Ed. White Plains, NY: Longman.

Dreikurs, R. (1957). *Psychology in the classroom.* New York: Harper & Row.

References

Edelman, G. (1987). *Neural Darwinism: The theory of neuronal group selection*. New York: Basic Books.

Education Department of South Australia. (1980). *Developing the classroom group: A manual for the inservice trainer*. Report No. 4. Adelaide, South Australia: Government Printer of South Australia.

Gardner, L. (1983). *Frames of mind: The theory of multiple intelligences*. New York: Basic Books.

Gathercoal, F. (2005). *Judicious Discipline*, 6th Ed. San Francisco: Caddo Gap Press.

Gathercoal, P., & Nimmo, V. (2002). Judicious discipline: Democracy in education. *Journal of Thought*, (Summer), 73-88.

Gathercoal, P. (2000). Conducting democratic class meetings. Paper presented at the Annual Meeting of the American Educational Research Association (New Orleans, LA, April 24-28). Eric, ED442736.

Gathercoal, P., & Crowell, R. (2000). Judicious discipline. *Kappa Delta Pi Record*, 36, 173-177.

Gathercoal, P. (1999). Judicious discipline and neuroscience: Constructing a neurological rationale for democracy in the classroom. In Barbara M. Landau (Ed.), *Practicing judicious discipline: An educator's guide to a democratic classroom* (3rd ed.) San Francisco: Caddo Gap Press.

Gathercoal, P. (1998). Educational leadership and judicious discipline. *Educational Leadership and Administration: Teaching and Program Development*, 10, 47-59.

Gathercoal, P., & Connolly, J. (1995). *Conducting democratic class meetings*. Produced and Directed by Paul Gathercoal. 20 min. Corroboree, LLC. Video.

Gathercoal, P., & Quin, R. (1993). On interactive media and hidden agendas. *Quarterly Journal of Ideology*, *16*(3 &4), 77-84.

Gathercoal, P. (1993, Nov. 20). Modern technology's dark side. *Chicago Tribune*, pp. 23.

Gathercoal, P. (1990). Brain research and mediated experience: An interpretation of the implications for education. *The Clearing House*, *63*(6), 271-273.

Goldstein, A. (1980). Thrills in response to music and other stimuli. *Physiological Psychology*, *8*(1), 126-129.

Grossberg, S. (1980). How does a brain build a cognitive code? *Psychological Review*, *87*(1), 1-39.

Holloway, M. (1992). Under construction: Temporary scaffolding guides nerves in the developing brain. *Scientific American*, *266*(1), 25-26.

Kandel, E. (1994). Genes, synapses, and memory. Paper presented at Nobel Conference on Neuroscience. Gustavus Adolphus College, St. Peter, MN.

Kandel, E., & Hawkins, R. (1992). The biological basis of learning and individuality. *Scientific American*, 79-86.

Kandel, E., Schwartz, J., & Jessell, T. (1991). *Principles of neural science*, 3rd Ed. New York: Elsevier.

Kehoe, P. (1988). Opioids, behavior, and learning in mammalian development. In E.M. Blass (Ed.), *Handbook of behavioral neurobiology: Volume 9: Developmental psychobiology and behavioral ecology* (pp. 309-346). New York: Plenum Press.

Kohlberg, L. (1976). Moral stages and moralization: The cognitive-developmental approach. In Thomas Lickora (Ed.), *Moral development and behavior*. New York: Holt, Rinehart & Winston.

Landau, B., & Gathercoal, P. (2000). Creating peaceful classrooms: *Judicious Discipline* and class meetings. *Phi Delta Kappan*, 81, 450-454.

Langer, E. (1989). *Mindfulness*. Reading, MA: Addison-Wesley.

Levinthal, C. (1990). *Introduction to physiological psychology*. Englewood Cliffs, NJ: Prentice Hall.

Levinthal, C. (1988). *Messengers of paradise: Opiates and the brain*. New York: Anchor Press.

Levitt, R., Stilwell, D., & Evers, T. (1978). Brief communication: Morphine and shuttlebox self-stimulation in the rat: Tolerance studies. *Pharmacology Biochemistry & Behavior*, *9*, 567-569.

Lipsitt, L. (1990). Learning processes in the human newborn. In A. Diamond (Ed.), *The development and neural bases of higher cognitive functions*. New York: The New York Academy of Sciences.

McAuliffe, K. (1985). Making of a mind. *Omni*, 74, 63-67.

McEwan, B., Gathercoal, P., & Nimmo, V. (1999). Application of *Judicious Discipline*: A common language for classroom management. In H. Jerome Freiberg (Ed.), *Beyond behaviorism: Changing the classroom management paradigm*. Boston: Allyn & Bacon.

Ornstein, R., & Thompson, R. (1984). *The amazing brain*. Boston: Houghton Mifflin.

Restak, R. (1994). *Receptors*. New York: Bantam Books.

Restak, R. (1992). See no evil: The neurological defense would blame violence on the damaged brain. *The Sciences*, 16-21.

Restak, R. (1988). *The mind*. New York: Bantam Books.

Rubinstein, E. (1983). Television and behavior: Research conclusions of the 1982 nimh report and their policy implications. *American Psychologist*, 820-825.

South Australian Council for Children's Films and Television, Inc. (1986). *Kids and the scary world of video*. A Study of Video Viewing Among 1498 Primary School Children in South Australia, published by the Television Committee of the South Australian Council for Children's Films and Television, Inc.

Smith, F. (1990). *To think*. New York: Teachers College Press.

Squire, L. (1987). *Memory and brain*. New York: Oxford University Press.

Sylwester, R. (1993). What the biology of the brain tells us about learning. *Educational Leadership*, *51*(4), 46-51

Sylwester, R. (1995). The neurobiology of self-esteem and aggression. *Educational Leadership*, *54*(5), 75-79

Sylwester, R. (1995). *A celebration of neurons: An educator's guide to the human brain*. Alexandria, VA: Association for Supervision and Curriculum Development.

Van Taylor, D. (1991). *Dream deceivers*. Produced and Directed by David Van Taylor.

Wheeler, D. (1992). An escalating debate over research that links biology and human behavior. *The Chronicle of Higher Education*, A7-A8.

About the Authors

Paul Gathercoal, Forrest's brother, is a professor and director of Curriculum and Instruction, Assessment, and Teaching with Technology in the School of Education at California Lutheran University in Thousand Oaks, California. Previously he has served as assistant professor of education at Gustavus Adolphus College in St. Peter, Minnesota, and as a teacher and project officer with the South Australian Education Department. Paul holds a B.S. degree in education from Southern Oregon College and M.Ed. and Ph.D. degrees in Curriculum and Instruction from the University of Oregon. He has authored or co-authored numerous articles and conference presentations on the effects of media on individuals and society, classroom management and school discipline, the implementation and use of webfolios in assessment, evaluation and reporting, integrating computer-based technology into teaching and learning, and several other educational topics.

Forrest Gathercoal, Paul's brother, is a professor emeritus in the College of Education at Oregon State University, Corvallis, Oregon, and an adjunct professor at Lewis and Clark College, Portland, Oregon. While at Oregon State University he was Assistant Dean and Professor in the College of Education. He taught educational psychology and continues to teach school law, conducts workshops on parenting and school discipline, presents frequently at educational conferences, and serves as a consultant to school districts, state education agencies, and colleges and universities across the United States. Previously, at the public school level, Forrest has been a music teacher, coach, counselor, and dean of boys. He holds two degrees from the University of Oregon, a bachelor's in music and a J.D. from the School of Law. Forrest is author of *Judicious Discipline*, a book which provides a framework for creating a democratic school environment, and the related books *Judicious Parenting*, which does the same for families, *A Judicious Philosophy for School Support Personnel*, *Judicious Coaching*, and *Judicious Leadership for Residence Hall Living*. He is co-author of *On Being the Boss* and *Legal Issues for Industrial Educators* and author of numerous magazine and journal articles.